GOLF

CROWOOD SPORTS GUIDES

GOLF

SKILLS

TRAINING

TECHNIQUES

Matt Stables

THE CROWOOD PRESS

First published in 2013 by
The Crowood Press Ltd
Ramsbury, Marlborough
Wiltshire SN8 2HR

www.crowood.com

British Library Cataloguing-in-Publication Data
A catalogue record for this book is available from the British Library.

ISBN 978 1 84797 531 7

Photographs by George Powell, www.gppics.com
Diagrams by Charlotte Kelly

Typeset by Jean Cussons Typesetting, Diss, Norfolk
Printed and bound in India by Replika Press Pvt Ltd

CONTENTS

PREFACE

Welcome to the *Crowood Sports Guide: Golf*. The aim of this book is to equip players of all abilities and experience with the tools to excel at golf and to enjoy the game. This book is aimed as much at the complete beginner who is just looking to start the game, as it is at experienced players who wish to take their skill to the next level. It is important to understand a number of different areas to play to your best, and many aspects will be looked at so that you have the tools to improve and enjoy this great game.

The first section will take you through the history of the game in the hope that the great players and golf's evolution will inspire you to play and understand the modern game. Then in Part Two we will describe the stages of getting started, the basics of the technique or the swing, then putting and the short game. This section is designed for the beginner – but even the more experienced should review the information contained herein, as there will be something to help even the most advanced player.

In Part Three we will cover more advanced swing ideas, and then discuss other areas that may have an impact on your performance and enjoyment of the game, such as to how to use your practice time, the mental game, how your equipment performs, and your fitness for golf. It will also cover subjects such as how to keep improving your swing, understanding how the body works, swing plane, and the correct impact position.

Each chapter will begin with a synopsis of the objectives discussed within it, and will then explain in more detail how these objectives might be achieved. Note that the text assumes that the player is right-handed. Left-handed players should simply reverse the terms.

PART I
INTRODUCTION TO THE GAME

CHAPTER 1

THE HISTORY OF THE GAME OF GOLF

In this section the objectives discussed are:

- To understand golf's beginnings
- To learn about the greats of the game in order to be inspired by, and to learn from them

The Early History of Golf

The game of golf has a long history, the first mention of a stick and ball game going back to the Netherlands in 1297, where the Dutch played a game with a stick and a leather ball with the aim of using the least number of strokes to get the ball to a target a few hundred yards away. And there is even evidence of some form of the game being played in China in around the year 1000AD. But the consensus is that the modern game evolved in Scotland, and that golf as it is today – played over eighteen holes – also originated in Scotland.

The first documented mention of golf in Scotland appears in an Act of the Scottish Parliament in 1457, when King James II of Scotland prohibited the playing of the games of 'gouf' and football, as these were a distraction from archery practice for military purposes. Bans were again imposed in Acts of 1471 and 1491, with golf being described as 'an unprofitable sport' and an unwanted distraction. Mary, Queen of Scots, was accused by her political enemies of playing golf after her second husband was murdered in 1567; George Buchanan subsequently wrote that she had been playing 'sports that were clearly unsuitable to women'.

Golf was banned again by parliament under King James VI of Scotland, but golf clubs and balls were bought for him in 1502 when he visited the home of golf, St Andrews in Scotland. The account book of a lawyer named Sir John Foulis of Ravelston records that he played golf at Musselburgh Links on 2 March 1672, suggesting that The Old Links, Musselburgh, is the oldest playing golf course in the world. There is also a story that Mary, Queen of Scots, played there in 1567, demonstrating that she was the first golfing celebrity of her time.

The Early Era 1860 to 1930

Golf started to become established as an international sport in the late nineteenth century, with over a thousand courses coming into existence in the UK. It also started to expand in the United States, with 267 clubs in 1910, and 1,100 clubs by 1930. Golf was truly on the rise and growing rapidly. The golf ball was also changing rapidly, because prior to 1930 there were numerous different types in use and it was continually evolving. The first balls used were called 'featheries' as they were made up of a stitched leather outer layer stuffed with feathers; however, due to the cost of manufacturing these golf balls they were replaced by gutta perca balls, which were made from the dried sap of a Malaysian Sapodilla tree. They developed from there into a ball with a liquid-filled core, which was surrounded by a layer of rubber thread and a thin outer layer. This was first developed by Coburn Haskell in the early 1900s, and this concept of a wound ball was developed and refined, and was still in use until the early twenty-first century.

The modern golf ball is made of several layers of different synthetic materials such as urethane. By using differing materials and layers, and with the aid of modern design technology, balls can have a variety of playing characteristics that will suit different players. The design process and quality control has improved, which has meant that balls are much more consistent in their performance, something that the early balls were not.

The current majors started to be played during this era, with the Open Championship in 1860 and the US Open in 1895. These helped to popularize the game and encouraged participation.

One of the great players of the era was Bobby Jones, who as an amateur won all the major tournaments of this time. In 1930 he completed the Grand Slam, when he won the US Open, the Open Championship, and the British Amateur and US Amateur championships. He also opened the Augusta National Golf Club, where he founded one of the modern majors, The Masters. Playing his first Open Championship at St Andrews in Scotland, he famously withdrew after eleven holes by tearing up his score card, stating that he didn't like links golf. Despite this he was well known for his sportsmanship both on and off the golf course. Ironically he won the Open Championship at St Andrews on his way to the Grand Slam in 1930.

Another great player of the era who helped popularize the game was Walter Hagen, famously playing numerous exhibition matches across the United States and around the world. He had an aggressive style of play and a love of tailored clothing, which helped raise the profile of professional golfers and the game.

1930 to 1960

During this period golfing equipment further developed, with the introduction of steel shafts in the clubs, replacing the wooden hickory shafts used previously. This meant that the swing began to evolve to cope with the different playing characteristics, as the steel shafts were more uniform in the way they played; they could be tailored for mass production, and modified to suit the individual.

The great players during this era were Ben Hogan, Sam Snead and Byron Nelson. Byron Nelson famously won eleven consecutive tournaments and eighteen events during 1945, with a stroke average of sixty-eight. This record remains to this day – his stroke average is similar to that of modern players, but considering he had inferior equipment as compared to today, and played on courses that were far less manicured, this only goes to demonstrate his ability.

Ben Hogan was a legendary ball striker known for his tremendous work ethic, as well as his ideas on how to swing. His book *The Five Fundamentals of Golf* has had a huge influence on the modern swing and coaching. He overcame much adversity during his life, starting with his father committing suicide when Hogan was a child. After struggling early on in his career, he continued to work hard and developed his technique. He was penniless a number of times and didn't win his first professional tournament until he was twenty-eight, ten years after he turned professional. In February 1949 he was involved in a car accident, which left him with a fractured pelvis, collar bone and left ankle, chipped rib and blood clots, from which he nearly died.

Despite this Hogan returned to the golf course within a year and went on to win the 1950 US Open. In 1953 he recorded one of the best seasons in professional golf, winning three of the four modern majors. He was not able to compete in the USPGA Championship, as the dates clashed with the Open Championship. His achievements were even more impressive insofar as the injuries he suffered affected him for the rest of his life. He is regarded as one of the greatest golfers of all time, and one of the best ball strikers. His determination and dedication to the game is something many players have tried to emulate.

Sam Snead is the last of this great threesome; he currently has the most wins on the PGA Tour with eighty-two, and was known as 'Slammin' Sam'. He possessed a great natural swing, which created seemingly effortless power, and was a natural athlete. He was the opposite of Ben Hogan, who worked so very hard to become a great player, and soon found his feet on the tour by winning five times during his first year. He had a long career, which could be attributed to his flexibility and fitness. He is the oldest player to win on the tour, at fifty-two years old, and his swing and his style of play were both natural and admired by many.

During the 1950s the game continued to develop and expand. Golf was broadcast on the television for the first time, which helped to bring its popularity to a wider audience. Magazines and news media coverage also helped to increase interest in the game.

1960 to the 1980s

In most eras of golf great players have come in threes, and heading into the next era these players would be Jack Nicklaus, Arnold Palmer and Gary Player. This threesome became known as the 'big three'. They all had different styles, and would excite the golf world throughout their careers. In the early sixties Arnold Palmer had emerged as the dominant golfer, whose attacking 'go for broke' style of play was admired and had won him an army of fans, affectionately known as 'Arnie's Army'.

Jack Nicklaus emerged at the US Open in 1962 and beat Arnold Palmer in a play-off to get his first win and major championship. This proved unpopular with Arnie's Army and was the beginning of a great rivalry that created a lot of interest in the game and helped increase its popularity. This was the beginning of Nicklaus going on to become the most successful golfer of all time: by the end of his playing career he had won two US amateur championships and eighteen professional major championships, plus seventy-six PGA Tour wins and eight major wins on the Senior Tour. He finished in the top three in major championships forty-six other times.

His consistency over many years can only be admired. His last major win came at the 1986 Masters, and is considered to be one of the greatest tournaments of all time. He marched through the back nine in thirty shots to win his eighteenth major. The biggest lesson we can all learn from Nicklaus was his mental game and course management.

Arnold Palmer was most dominant from 1960 to 1963, before Nicklaus arrived on the pro scene, but he continued to win numerous tournaments and also won seven professional majors. He popularized the Open Championship in Britain with the top American professionals, because at that time they didn't want to travel to play in the tournament. Palmer won the tournament in 1961 and 1962, raising international interest in the event. He was intent on being a world player, as opposed to just focusing on the American circuit.

His popularity did a huge amount to increase golf's support, which meant the growth of professional golf continued. He played without fear, and was always aggressive, which made his style fun to watch. His charisma took golf to a new level as he created a lot of interest in the game, in much the same way that Tiger Woods has done in recent times.

Gary Player was one of the most travelled athletes in history, and has always possessed great enthusiasm and drive for everything he does. He was a major advocate of being fit, and was one of the first golfers to use fitness as a way to improve his performance. This is something we can learn a great deal from. His career was not as long as those of Nicklaus and Palmer, but he made up for it in determination, mental strength, a great short game and hard work. He won nine major championships and six Senior

Tour majors, and had over 120 professional wins. He was also a great ambassador for South Africa during a difficult time in its history, and was voted sportsman of the century in his home country – he even had his face on a stamp. He estimates that he has travelled over 15 million miles in his career in his desire to be a world player and to popularize golf around the world.

Each of the big three has left a considerable legacy to the game, including traits we can learn from them. In particular they are responsible for the design of numerous courses around the world: Gary Player and Jack Nicklaus have each been involved in over 300 course design projects, and Palmer over 250. These courses are all over the world, and will ensure that people keep playing and enjoying the game for many years in the future. These three players have also inspired many with their skill, sportsmanship and love of the game.

1980 to the mid-1990s

Into the 1980s the big three were still playing, but a new wave of golfers came to the fore. American players were leading the way, but there were also some great players emerging in Europe. There was a belief that American players were superior to the Europeans, and this was demonstrated in the Ryder Cup. The Ryder Cup was founded as a biennial match for professional golfers played between the USA and Great Britain and Ireland. Up until 1977 the USA had won twenty-one out of twenty-four of the matches played, and ten in a row. To make the matches more competitive, in 1979 it was decided that from then on they would include Europe as well. One man in particular was to prove inspirational in changing the balance of power in these matches, namely Severiano Ballesteros. Seve, as he was affectionately known, was becoming a great player, having won the Open Championship in 1979 and the Masters in 1980.

He had a very distinctive style of play.

He was not always the straightest player off the tee, but he was able to recover in spectacular fashion most of the time, and had a great short game. He turned pro at fifteen, and learnt the game with a 3 iron by practising on the beach near his home in Santander, Spain. He used to build his own course on the beach, and would use his imagination to play all different types of shot. The result of this was that he could produce different types of shot, and had a great feel for the short game. He also possessed an undeniable will to win, and a respectful love of beating the Americans.

The match versus the Americans in 1983 proved to be a turning point in the Ryder Cup. The match was won by the Americans, but this match was the closest it had been in a number of years. Nick Faldo says that Seve walked into a despondent dressing room and said that it proved they were beatable. This new-found belief carried over to the next match, where Europe won at the Belfry. The momentum continued to build, and in 1987 Europe won the Ryder Cup for the first time on American soil, with Seve suitably holing the winning putt.

This match symbolized a great new era in European golf, with great players winning the world's biggest tournaments. Seve would win five majors, and Nick Faldo would be on his way to becoming the best English golfer of all time, winning six majors. Sandy Lyle and Bernhard Langer would win two majors each, and Ian Woosnam won the Masters in 1991. These five golfers would be Europe's big five players of their generation, and would continue to be instrumental for Europe both in the Ryder Cup and in winning tournaments around the world.

An official world ranking system was introduced in 1986. There were other great players during this period, notably Greg Norman and Tom Watson. Greg Norman has great charisma, and his style of play was aggressive and explosive. He was one of the greatest drivers of a golf ball. He won the Open Championship twice, as well as ninety professional wins all around the world; he has also become

a very successful businessman away from golf. He is best known for his near misses in the majors, and was unlucky on several occasions, as well as hitting some poor shots at the wrong time. In 1986 Bob Tway holed a bunker shot on the last hole to beat him, and in 1987 Larry Mize holed an outrageous chip across the green on the second play-off hole to beat him in the Masters.

He was also a victim in PGA Tour events when Robert Gamez holed his second shot from 187 yards to beat him on the last hole at Bay Hill, and David Frost holed from a bunker to beat him in New Orleans. He led all four major championships going into the last day in 1986, but only won one of them. He also let a number of tournaments slip through his fingers, particularly the 1996 Masters when he had a six shot lead going into the final round before surrendering to magnificent play by Nick Faldo. He could have won many more majors, especially the Masters – but all in all he had an outstanding career, and during its course was ranked world number one for 331 weeks.

Tom Watson was a great all-round player. He won eight major championships from the late 1970s, and enjoyed five wins in the British Open where he was especially good at handling the bad weather and seemed to love the conditions. In 1977 he had one of his great duels with Jack Nicklaus at Turnberry in Scotland. Both played exceptional golf, and were well in front of the rest of the field on the final day. Watson hit the ball to a few feet on the last hole to beat Nicklaus by one shot: this tournament became known as 'the duel in the sun'. Watson went on to win over seventy events and six senior majors.

In 2009 he returned to Turnberry at the age of fifty-nine for the Open. He led until the last hole, needing a par for victory. On his second shot he hit it very much like he did in 1977: straight at the flag, but a firm bounce carried it through the green, and a missed 8ft putt resulted in a bogey. He lost in the play-off to Stewart Cink, and left everyone disappointed that he didn't win a record sixth Open championship and become the oldest winner of a major championship.

As well as the above great players of the game, there were numerous others making their mark. Payne Stewart was much loved; known for wearing plus fours and for his smooth languid swing, he won three majors, including the US Open in 1999. He was tragically killed in a plane crash later that year.

1996 to the Modern Day

In 1996 Tiger Woods turned professional after winning three consecutive US amateur championships. He quickly made his mark by winning two tournaments, and then in 1997 he won his first major, The Masters, by twelve shots. He dominated fields by hitting the ball further and straighter than had ever been seen before, and displayed excellence in all areas of the game.

His biggest influence on the game was his conviction that to be a successful golfer you had to be an athlete, and his superior fitness level was a tremendous asset. Besides this he really was an excellent all-round player, and always excited the golfing audience – television viewing numbers always increased when he was playing. He would go on to dominate golf with a standard of play that was exceptional. Up until 2009 he won fourteen majors, and was 'player of the year' ten times in twelve years. He created excitement each time he played, and hit many great shots when he needed to.

He was trained from a young age by his father Earl, and won numerous events first at junior level, then as an amateur, and then professionally. He used Jack Nicklaus as a model, and together they set the aim of beating Nicklaus' record of winning eighteen professional majors. In 2001 he won The Masters, meaning that he held all four major tournaments at the same time. This had not been achieved before in the modern era, and was dubbed the 'Tiger Slam'. Although the wins were not achieved in the same season, it is still seen as the greatest achievement since Bobby Jones' Grand Slam in 1930. Despite fitness issues and personal problems that started at the end of 2009 and continued through 2010, he continues in his quest to beat Nicklaus' record.

During this time there have been several advances in the use of technology. Golf ball design changed from a wound core to a new multi-layer construction of synthetic materials, which meant the ball would go further; it could also be manipulated to produce a different spin and feel, resulting in better performance. Today's players are aided by computer-designed equipment and better materials; also clubs can be designed to fit the individual player, which in theory makes the game easier for the average player, and improves performance at professional level.

Furthermore the development of launch monitors, which track the golf ball's spin and trajectory, as well as club path and face angle at impact, give great feedback as to a player's swing specifications. Wider options of club-head design and more choice of golf shafts has meant that clubs can be more easily fitted to players at all levels of the game. This technology has also aided designers in developing clubs.

The improvements in club and ball technology have resulted in players hitting the ball longer distances. Many courses, including those used for championships, have been made longer, and new courses have been designed with length in mind. Tiger Woods has inspired a new generation into golf, who see that golfers now have to be athletes, meaning that many players are stronger and more flexible and are consequently able to hit the ball further. Coaching has also changed, with the development of new technology to measure player performance; this has meant that players have more and better information to work on to improve their game. More effective programmes can therefore be drawn up to develop fitness, club fitting, swing technique, short game coaching, nutrition, psychology and lifestyle, all of which help to maximize their performance.

In Conclusion

The game of golf continues to grow and develop, with continuing advancements and great players past and present as inspiration. Golf remains one of the world's most popular sports, and thanks to its great history and the people who support it, this will continue for many years to come. Each of the great players described in this chapter has made a great contribution to the game: there is something to be learnt from each one of them, and something to inspire us, and by understanding how the game has developed, we can have a greater appreciation of their legacy.

PART 2

THE BASIC TOOLS

THE AIM OF THE GAME

In this chapter the objectives discussed are:

- How to get started in the game, and how to get involved
- Understanding what equipment you need
- Finding out where you can play

The basic aim of golf is to hit the ball from the tee into the hole in as few shots as possible, over a course with eighteen holes, and to do this with the lowest score possible. It sounds simple, but as Arnold Palmer once said, 'Golf is deceptively simple and endlessly complicated.' This is different from many other sports where the goal is to get more points or goals. In golf, less is more.

In many sports you are faced with a direct opponent or opposition team. This is also true in competitive golf; however, you are also faced with the distinct challenges of the golf course, the weather conditions, and your own mental state. Golf also has a high level of sportsmanship as there is generally no referee and the rules are administered by the people playing. The spirit of the game is one of honesty, integrity and courtesy, which is something that golfers value highly.

Equipment

This section investigates what you need to get started, and your different options. Golf is perceived as an expensive sport, but it doesn't have to be when you first start. There is no need to spend a small fortune on buying top of the range equipment – if you are not sure whether you will play the game a lot you can start with just one or two clubs to discover if you enjoy it and if you do want to take it

further. But beware – generally it takes only a few good shots to ensure that you become hooked!

Your options are as follows:

To get one iron and a putter: Many golf shops will sell you individual clubs that are relatively inexpensive. You will want to get a 7, 8 or 9 iron as these are the 'game improver' clubs: they are the easier clubs to hit as they are not long and have enough loft to help get the ball into the air. Also a putter will mean you can start to develop a very important part of the game.

To get a package set: Another option is to get a package set of clubs, as this will provide you with everything you will need: irons, woods, putter and bag. This will vary between different sets and manufacturers, but it is a very cost-effective way of getting everything that you need to play. These sets are often not of great quality, and as you play more you may want to upgrade, but they are sufficient at the beginner stage.

To buy a second-hand set: You could buy a second-hand set, but make sure the clubs are designed for a beginner: a great deal is of no benefit if they are the incorrect specification for you. It is advisable to choose clubs that are designed for game improvement, such as a perimeter-weighted club head with a large cavity and enough flexibility in the shaft of the club. Also, ensure the grips are not worn out; if they are, have them regripped by a PGA professional.

To rent a set: Most golf facilities will let you borrow clubs or rent a set for the round. There will usually be a charge for this, and the quality of clubs you get will

vary. Also, you will not be able to get used to how a club plays. Be sure to check that the golf facility has this option before you go.

Unless you go to a driving range you will need to provide your own balls, tees, appropriate clothing and shoes.

What to Wear

Golf has its own etiquette regarding what you should wear, due to the traditional nature of the game. Dress codes have become more relaxed in recent years, and each facility will be different in its requirements, but generally it is advisable to observe the following dress code:

- Avoid wearing denim
- Wear a collared shirt
- Smart trainers are fine if you don't have golf shoes
- Wear smart trousers if possible, but check before you go: you will need these if you go to a private course

How to Get Involved

There are a number of ways you can become involved in golf. Once you have got some equipment, then you will have to choose where you are going to play. Below are some of your options:

- **Driving range:** A great place to learn how to hit the ball and develop your swing.
- **Pitch and putt/par 3 course:** A short course where you can learn how to play short shots and to putt.
- **Public course:** A course where anyone can play, but check the course

difficulty as you may not want to venture straight on to a full course as a beginner.

- **Beginners' groups:** Learn the basics of the game and meet like-minded golfers.
- **Lessons with a PGA professional:** Learn the basics of the game on a one-to-one basis.

Even though golf is an individual game, players will find it more enjoyable if they embrace its social side. This may mean learning with a friend or introducing yourself to other people at the golf course, or asking your PGA professional to introduce you to a player of similar ability. This will make the learning process more enjoyable. Remember, too, that there are always other golfers who are in the same situation and looking for a playing partner, so don't be too apprehensive as you are not alone in this regard.

Basic Etiquette

In golf there are some basic rules of etiquette that should be followed,:

- The maximum number of players in each group should be four; any more and this really slows down play.
- For safety reasons stand well behind the player who is hitting the ball, as there is always a possibility that a mis-hit shot will go in a strange direction, and being hit by a fast moving golf ball may cause serious injury.
- Shout 'fore' if you hit the ball towards another player to warn them that a ball is coming towards them. 'Fore' is the recognized term in golf, and other players will recognize this as a warning to get out of the way or to protect their heads.
- Let faster players play through: if there is a group of players behind you who are waiting for you, please stand aside and let them play through.
- Ensure you are ready to play when it is your turn.

- Replace your divots and rake the bunkers: a well conditioned course makes the game easier, and all golfers need to help the green keepers look after the course.

Finding a Coach

Whether you are learning the game from scratch, coming back to it, or simply want to improve, the best and quickest way to achieve your goals is to find a coach. This will save you a lot of time and endless frustration, as golf is a difficult game to learn. It is different to the learning process for many other sports such as football or rugby, where you learn the basics of the game simply by doing it. In golf it is essential that you learn the correct fundamentals of the game right from the beginning, due to the mechanical complexities of the golf swing. This will mean that you can ingrain good habits rather than bad ones: bad habits are much harder to correct after you have played for a while, and many players find they hit a wall where they don't improve due to ingrained bad habits.

Make sure the coach is PGA qualified: The Professional Golfers Association (PGA) is the governing body of professional golfers in Great Britain, Ireland and around the world, and a PGA-qualified professional will have had a high level of training in all parts of the game. Your learning process will therefore be in good hands.

Have an introductory session: Most coaches will offer a discounted introductory lesson where you will meet with them and identify a plan of improvement. This will give you the opportunity to make sure their style of coaching suits you, and you will both be able to get to know each other to discuss how best to proceed.

Learning as a beginner: As a beginner your aim will be to learn good fundamentals in all areas of the game. You will want to learn the basics of the set-up,

how to make a good contact, adopt a good finish position, how to putt, and so on. This is important, because if you start with bad basics they will be much harder to correct further down the line.

Improving as an experienced player: As an experienced player you will want to identify your strengths and weaknesses so that you can understand why your game has not been improving as you would have liked. You will then need to understand why these issues are not helping your game, and what the process is to correct the problem.

Practise what you have been taught: It is important that when learning you take some time in between lessons to practise what you have been working on. You don't have to spend a lot of time on this – just ten minutes in the garden practising your swing is very helpful to consolidate what you have been learning. Practising at the range or on the course is even better. No one ever achieved any improvement in anything without practice.

Work on one thing at a time: You don't have to get everything correct straight away. If you get better by concentrating on just one thing at a time, this will add up over time and result in great progress. Think how a house is built: one brick at a time, and in the same way once you have mastered one thing you can move on to the next.

Be patient: Whether learning the game or trying to make improvements, remember golf can be a difficult game at times. Be patient when working to acquire a new move or skill. It will take time for the changes to become ingrained, and for a time you may not see the results you would like. But remain committed to the process and you will be pleasantly surprised.

Ask questions: If there is something that you don't understand, or you are not seeing the result that you are looking for, ask your coach for a different view and give them your feedback.

CHAPTER 3

THE SET-UP FOR THE SWING

In this chapter the objective discussed is:

• To learn the fundamentals of the set-up: this is the beginning of a great swing

The Set-up

The set-up is where all good swings start, as there are key fundamentals that will make a successful swing more likely to happen. If you set up correctly it will mean that you won't have to make compensations later in the swing, and you can develop good swing habits. Many faults start in the set-up, and even top professionals check their own regularly. The elements of a good set-up are easily

remembered by the acronym G.A.S.P., which stands for:

G. Grip
A. Aim
S. Stance
P. Posture

Grip

Jack Nicklaus said that good golf starts with a good grip. It is your only contact with the club, and a good grip will allow you to have effective control of the clubface at impact, and will help to create power and to give a feel and touch for the game. If the grip is incorrect a player will have to make compensations to get the club square at impact, which is more complicated to do.

The Left-hand Grip
To start, hold the club out in front of you at chest height. We do this because it is much easier to view the grip as compared to trying to do it when the club is on the ground, where most players will struggle to adjust it. Hold the steel of the club just

Stance.

Grip.

Aim.

Posture.

Get your grip by holding the club in front of you at chest height.

In the left hand make sure the grip runs through the bottom part of your hand.

Once the left hand is in place, add the right hand by having the steel in the bottom crease of the fingers.

Bring the right hand down the grip, close your right hand, and make a V with your thumb and forefinger.

Put the club down on the ground and you have the grip.

below the grip with your right hand (if you are a right-handed golfer). From there, put your left hand on the club as if you would shake hands. Ensure your thumb goes on the club slightly right of centre, and the grip runs through the bottom part of your hand just above the base of your fingers.

Adding the right hand: Once the left hand is on, open your right hand so that the shaft is in the bottom crease of your fingers. Then bring your right hand down the grip and close your hand so that the thumb of the left hand goes into the lifeline of your right hand. The right thumb and index finger form a V shape. This is very important as there is a pressure point in the first knuckle joint of the right hand which will help you apply pressure to the back of the ball during the swing. Then the thumb goes slightly to the left and there is a gap between your first finger and index finger on the underside of the grip.

The overlapping grip, with the little finger of the left hand sitting on top of the gap between the index finger and the little finger.

The interlocking grip, where the index finger and little finger interlock.

The baseball grip.

Overlapping Grip, Interlocking Grip and Baseball Grip

There are a number of options in how the hands work together for the grip. When the hands come together this refers to how the little finger of the right hand and the index finger of the left hand connect. It is personal preference as to which one you use, but I would only recommend using the baseball grip if you are a beginner.

Overlapping grip: The little finger of the right hand sits on top of the gap between the index finger and the middle finger of the left hand. This is the most popular grip, and allows both hands to work together.

Interlocking grip: The little finger of the left hand and the index finger of the right hand interlock. This gives a more connected grip, and is usually preferred by players with smaller hands. When using this grip be careful to ensure that the fingers are *lightly* interlocked together and

not deep and tight, as this would make it harder to get the correct right-hand grip.

Baseball grip: The fingers do not interlock and the little finger and index fingers sit together. This is an acceptable grip for a beginner, but makes it more difficult for the hands to work together. The previous two grips will help the hands to work together better in the long term.

Checkpoints for your Grip

Check the Vs: The Vs or creases formed between your thumb and index finger on both hands should point at the seam of the right shoulder. You can easily check this when you are holding the club at hip height as the Vs will be apparent.

Thumb position: The thumbs should be slightly off centre, with the left-hand thumb (for a right-hander) slightly to the right and the right hand slightly to the left.

The Vs of both hands point to the seam of the right shoulder.

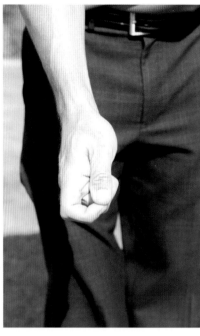

Make a peephole with the right hand to get the correct index finger and thumb position.

A common error is that the thumbs are both held straight down – this causes a weak grip where the club will tend to be open. The Vs formed in your grip will not point to your right shoulder and it will also mean the pressure points are not correct. Again check your thumb position when you are holding the club at hip height.

Make a peephole with your bottom hand: As an exercise to get the bottom hand position correct, take your bottom hand and make a peephole between your index finger and thumb. The shape of your thumb and index finger is the same shape that you are trying to make in your grip. Notice that there is a gap between your index finder and middle finger.

Grip pressure: Hold the club softly so that you have a feel for the shot. You should be able to move the club freely in your hands and make a circular motion with it when it is at hip height. A tight grip pressure will inhibit you swinging freely

To get the correct grip pressure you should be able to move the club around freely.

and will slow the club head down, which will cost you distance. Another way to gauge grip pressure is to think of it as being on a scale of one to ten, with ten being as hard as you can and one as light as possible. You want to be holding at about three or four, whereas many golfers hold it at eight or nine.

Pressure points: Remember we want the overall grip to be soft, and also there are some points of the grip that apply more pressure on the club than others. In the left hand, more pressure is felt in the last three fingers (middle finger, ring finger and little finger), with the index finger and the thumb being relaxed. In the right hand both middle two fingers (middle finger and ring finger) apply the pressure, with the index finger and thumb being relaxed.

A common error is where the pressure is applied through the thumb and index finger. Another key pressure point is the first knuckle joint of the index finger of the right hand. This pressure point is going to apply pressure to the back of the club for a downward strike through impact. If these pressure points are correct they will promote good use of the wrists throughout the stroke/swing.

Drill
To establish the pressure points in the left and right hand, hold the club in your left hand and take your thumb and index

finger off the club so that you are just holding it by the last three fingers of the left hand. This will give you the feeling of where the pressure should be applied.

Grip the club in your left hand and feel the pressure points of the last three fingers.

To feel the pressure points in the middle two fingers take your thumb and forefinger off the club.

Now, put your left thumb and index finger back on the club. Take your grip with your right hand. Now take the right index finger and thumb off the club. This will help you feel the middle two fingers (middle finger and ring finger) applying the pressure, and will take the pressure out of the thumb and index finger. Make some practice swings doing this.

Common Errors

Grip is too weak: The hands are too far to the left on the club and the Vs will point more to your right ear or to your nose; this encourages an open clubface to your target line at impact, and you will hit shots to the right of target.

Grip is too strong: The opposite effect is to place your hands too far to the right of the grip, when the Vs will point too far to the right of your shoulder. This encourages the clubface to close at impact, causing shots to the left of target. Being a little bit strong is not a bad thing, but this may need addressing if the ball goes to the left of target.

Grip pressure is too tight: If the grip pressure is too tight it will not let the wrists work correctly: they won't be able to hinge correctly on the backswing, and then unhinge correctly on the forward swing. If the grip is tight it will spread up the arms and create too much tension in the swing. This will inhibit a free-flowing swing and won't let you create club-head speed for power; it will also affect the consistency of strike. You can see when someone is gripping too hard as the hands and arms will appear very tense.

Gripping too much with the thumb and index finger: If the pressure is applied to the club with the index finger and thumb this will cause many of the same problems as with the grip being too tight. You will find it difficult to keep the wrist hinge into the downswing, and this could cause you to 'come over the top'. Try the drill

Too much pressure in the thumb and index finger.

described above to get the pressure points correct.

Aim

If you are not aimed correctly your best swing won't hit the ball to your target, and you will have to make a compensation to get it to go to there. The main problem with aiming is that you are standing to the side of the ball as opposed to, say, snooker when you are looking directly down the line you want to hit. The key concept to understand in order to aim correctly is that your feet, knees, hips and shoulders have to be aligned parallel to you target line. If you stand directly behind your ball and draw a line from the ball to the target, this is your target line. You then need to set yourself up with your body parallel to that line.

Grip is too weak.

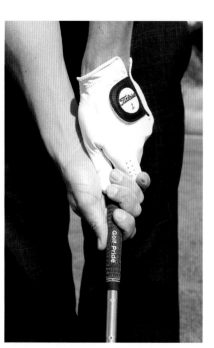

Grip is too strong.

Ways to Check your Alignment

Here are some easy ways to check that you are lined up correctly. You may like one of these methods, or you can use a combination to ensure you are aiming at the target each time.

Practise with a club on the ground:
When you go to the driving range to practise, put a club, an alignment stick or some other straight edge on the ground so that you have a reference point to help you aim correctly. Stand behind looking down the target line to ensure it is aimed correctly. Alignment sticks are made of fibreglass and are available from most pro shops. Many players have these in their bags for this reason.

Good alignment is when your feet, knees, hips and shoulders are aligned parallel to your target.

Put the club on the ground to make sure you are lined up correctly.

Put the club across your thighs to check your alignment.

Check how you look up at the target.

Put the club across your thighs: The great teacher Harvey Penick recommended this way to help your alignment. When you are set up, put the club across your thighs – you then move this out to the target line. You will easily see if you are standing parallel to the target line. This is a great way to check alignment when you are on the course.

Check how you look up at the target: When you are setting up to the ball, focus on how you turn your head to look at the target. You want to just swivel your head, and you should be looking at your target. If you feel you have to look over your shoulder to see your target, you are aiming to the right. Get used to just swivelling your head this way so that you train your eyes to get used to what correct aim looks like.

Have a friend check for you: Have a friend look from behind you to give you some feedback about where you are aiming. You can then make adjustments.

Drill

Line up to ten different targets and check your alignment each time, then use one of the methods above to check your alignment. By changing target each time you will test how well you are aiming, because this will simulate playing on the course where you will have to aim at a different target each time. If you are on the driving range it is easy to get lazy and just line up to where the range mat is pointing you, and what happens on the course is that you end up lining up along the tee line, which often doesn't aim where you intend to go. Pick targets to the right and left on the driving range.

Stance

The stance is how your feet stand to the ball. The main purpose of the stance is to give you a stable base from which to make a swing at the ball.

Check how you line up to ten different targets.

The Width of Stance

The width of your stance should be a little more than the width of your shoulders. To check this, if you drop the club down from the seam of your shoulder it should point down to the inside of your foot; this will allow for people who are of different builds. The width stays fairly constant with all your clubs, though your stance will be just a little narrower – maybe an inch – with your wedges, and slightly wider by an inch or so with your driver. A wider stance with the driver is necessary so that the spine may tilt away from the ball, thus putting you in a position to sweep the ball from the tee as well as providing increased stability for the higher club-head speed created by the longer shaft.

Ball Position

The ball position is where the ball is in relation to your feet. To check this, put a club or an alignment stick on the ground, and the ball position needs to be just before your club reaches the bottom of your arc: this will be halfway between the middle of your stance and the left heel. You can measure this easily by measuring one-and-a-half club heads' width from your left heel. This will give you a good idea where to position the ball, but you can check this once you are making a correct swing by seeing where the club strikes the ground.

Shoulder-width stance.

The ball position does change slightly for different clubs, and there are differing theories about where it should be. Jack Nicklaus used to advocate that each ball position should be off the left heel for every shot, but very few tour players do this. Most modern players use the following three ball positions:

*   For hybrids through to a 9 iron: one-and-a-half club heads inside your left heel
*   For a driver and fairway woods: one club head inside your left heel
*   For wedges, chips and pitches: in the centre of the stance

The ball will be placed progressively further back for shorter clubs as you want a more descending blow, and slightly further forward with the woods as you want to sweep these a bit more. However, the ball position does not change dramatically and it is only a slight change, depending on the club being used. This makes it simpler to be placed correctly for each shot.

Posture

What you are trying to achieve with your posture is an athletic position where you are ready to make the motion that is the golf swing. You want to stand to the ball as you would if you were making any other move, such as jumping into a swimming pool or being a goalkeeper ready to save a penalty. You want to be on the balls of your feet, have some live tension in your thighs, and have your back fairly straight with your shoulders back and bending from the waist. If your posture is correct, your distance from the ball will be correct with every club. Although each club is a different length and the actual distance you are from the ball is different with each club, your posture shape will be the same.

Try the following different methods to establish a perfect posture with every club in the bag.

Ball position for hybrids through to a 9 iron.

Ball position for a driver and 3 wood.

Ball position for wedges, chips and pitches.

Start with the club out in front of you, and bend forwards from the waist.

Club out in front and bend forwards: Take your grip and hold the club out in front of you parallel to the ground; then bend forwards from the waist until the club reaches the ground. It is very important that you bend from the waist and not from the torso. Where the club lands will indicate your distance from the ball.

Bend forwards and let your hands clap together: Lean your club on your thighs, then bend forwards from the waist and clap your hands together. Your hands should hang in a natural position under your sternum. Then take your grip without moving too much.

Bend forwards and clap your hands together.

Club behind your back with hands on the club: This is a good exercise if you struggle to keep your back in the correct posture because it encourages you to pinch your shoulder blades together, which is characteristic of good posture. What happens when your back is rounded, which is bad posture, is that your shoulder blades are too far apart. If you put a club behind you at the bottom of your spine and then put your hands in an open position with your palms on the club, you will feel your shoulder blades pinch together. Hold this position for 10 to 20 seconds and really get a feel for how your shoulder blades feel. Then bring the club round in front of you and take your grip while you keep your posture position. You should feel as if you are in a really athletic position.

Let the right hand swing off and swing back in: This is a really good check for your distance from the ball and your hand position. When you are in your address position, let your right hand swing off the club and back in again. You shouldn't consciously control what your arm is doing, you should just let it swing backwards and forwards without thinking about it too much. If your hand swings back into the same position it was in to begin with, you are the correct distance from the ball. If it doesn't come back to the same position, this tells you that you need to adjust your distance from the ball, or your hand position.

Does your Everyday Posture Affect your Golf Posture?

It is important to appreciate that your posture in everyday life will affect your golf posture. If you have a slumped or rounded posture in your normal day-to-day life it is much more difficult to make a golf swing with a good athletic posture. In modern life we spend a great deal of time in front of computers or televisions, or have office-based jobs which encourage us to have poor posture, which means

Putting the club behind your back will encourage you to pinch your shoulder blades together.

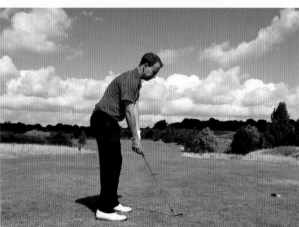

Let the right had swing off to check that you are the correct distance away.

that to help your golf you may have to address physical issues as well. Many fitness professionals will offer you postural screening where they will identify any issues you may have with obtaining a good posture, and will then give you a correctional programme of some basic exercises to improve this. By doing this you help your golf, and you will also look after your back and feel much better as well. Be sure to consult your doctor before you embark on any exercise programme.

Bad everyday posture will affect your golf posture.

CHAPTER 4

STRIKING THE BALL AND BUILDING THE SWING

In this chapter the objectives discussed are as follows:

- Why making good contact comes first, before distance and accuracy
- Starting to develop a good contact
- Developing the foundations of a good swing

Understanding Good Contact

It is important to understand what good contact is, and why it comes before distance and accuracy.

The first element of a good golf shot is to strike the ball correctly, because without a correct contact you won't be able to achieve distance and accuracy consistently. The elements of good contact include striking the ball in the centre of the clubface, and the bottom third of the ball with a descending blow. If you hit with the heel or the toe of the club you won't get the result you would like, and you will not transfer enough

energy to the ball to get its full distance. Conversely, if you strike the ball correctly you will get an effortless feeling and a soft clip sound, which means you have compressed the ball against the clubface so that it will have maximum energy. The sound of the strike will give you great feedback as to how well you have made contact, and is something each player should pay attention to.

Remember: golf is a game of opposites. To get the ball into the air you must hit down on it slightly.

Hitting off the toe.

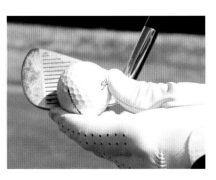

This is good contact.

Hitting off the heel.

The Mini Swing and Keeping the Triangle

One of the keys to great ball striking is to have a firm left wrist at impact for the right-handed player. If you look at all the great players, you will see that they all have this in common despite having radically different swing styles. This is an imperative of an effective golf swing, and is something that players need to start developing as soon as possible in their golfing careers – most people will do the opposite and try to scoop the ball in the air, which means the left wrist is breaking down. This is a very hard pattern of movement to change.

A great way to picture this and to try to develop it is to 'keep the triangle'. This is where the shape formed by the arms at address is kept when making a mini swing. By just keeping the triangle you will be developing the skill of being able to strike the ball.

Drill: Mini Swings Keeping the Triangle: If you work on this mini swing exercise by hitting shots 20 to 30 yards from a full swing, set up and just work on making good contact and keeping the triangle. To start with, work on this by hitting from a tee, and as you are more successful you will be able to move down to a lower tee and then the ground. Make sure you hold your finish to check if you have kept the triangle – and listen to the sound of the strike, because you will hear very quickly if you have done it correctly. You will also want to try doing practice swings, where you are just brushing the grass.

Mini swing keeping the triangle of the arms.

Common Mistakes

Scooping the ball into the air: If you are scooping the ball into the air, the first thing to understand is that to get the ball airborne you must hit *down* on it slightly, and not try to lift it into the air. Signs that you are doing this are that the left wrist breaks down by bending on the mini swing and chip shots, your weight finishes on your back foot, and just after impact you will see your left arm break down. This will result in a lot of mis-hit shots where you hit the top of the ball, plus shots that will not have the power or effortless strike needed. To work on this, remember the triangle, and practise the above. This is a very common mistake, and it is not an easy pattern of movement to break.

The triangle breaking down and trying to scoop the ball into the air.

Swinging L to L.

Developing the Three-Quarter Swing

L to L Swing

Once you are striking the ball correctly with the half swing, the next step is to make it longer and progress to a three-quarter swing, where the left arm is parallel to the ground on the backswing and the right is parallel to the ground on the follow-through. A good way to picture the position you are trying to achieve is to think of swinging L to L: this is where the left arm and the club form an L shape on the backswing, which is mirrored on the follow-through. This will help you to achieve the correct wrist hinge on the backswing and to release the club correctly on the follow-through. Once this is correct you will be able to get into a good position at the top of the backswing.

The L on the backswing will show you if you have enough or too much wrist hinge: you are looking for approximately a 90-degree angle between your left arm and the club when the arm is parallel to the ground. On the follow-through you are aiming to mirror the L shape. When the right arm is parallel to the ground, the club should be pointing upwards, but this angle should be slightly more than 90 degrees. This shows that you have released the club correctly.

Drill: Grip down to check the Ls: Choke down on your club so that the grip is showing above the top of your left hand, because this will help to give a clear visual indicator as to how well you are creating the Ls in your swing. Aim to have the grip pointing downwards when the left arm is parallel to the ground on the backswing, and then mirror that on the through swing.

Gripping down the club to work on the L swings.

Using too much wrist on the backswing.

The left arm is too high on the follow-through.

Drill: Slow swings using a mirror: Work on this by checking your L positions in a mirror, or video your swing and check these positions. Rehearse the Ls by making half-speed swings so that you train yourself to achieve the correct position automatically.

Common Mistakes

Picking up the club with the wrists on the backswing: If you just use your wrists to take the club back, the L shape won't be formed and there won't be any distance between your chest and hands. This is a very weak position, and one that won't allow you to create any power. If you find yourself doing this, swing back to the three-quarter position and push your hands away from your body so there is a gap between your chest and your hands.

Chicken wing with the left arm through the swing: Here the left arm breaks down through the shot and the arm is very high on the way through. This is a sign that the club has not released, and you will struggle with a slice that curves a long way to the right, as this move makes it difficult to square the club at impact. This problem starts with the triangle breaking down earlier in the through swing, and you should first work on getting the triangle working through the shot better.

   You can take this to another stage by trying to get the left arm working lower on the way through. What you want to see is the left arm being covered by the right on the way through, and the arms being more level. If you see too much of the left arm from the front view you will be struggling with a slice.

CHAPTER 5

PUTTING

In this chapter the objectives discussed are as follows:

- Becoming competent at the most important part of the game
- Learning from the hole backwards to see success from the start
- Learning fun skills tests to play and compete with on the putting green

Putting is often referred to as the game within the game, and comprises approximately 40 per cent of the shots that you will play during a round of golf, whatever the level you play at. Tour players usually average twenty-nine putts per round when they are averaging rounds of seventy shots, whereas the player scoring a hundred will have about forty to fifty putts per round. So it is a major part of the game, where you can quickly improve your scores irrespective of your ability to strike the ball. Putting will allow you to take advantage of your good shots and help you recover from your bad shots.

Exercise for the experienced player:
Go through your last round and work out how many putts you had: this will give you an idea of what level your putting is currently at. How did this compare with what you thought it would be? If you want to go into more detail, note whether your first putt was either long or short of the hole, and how many times you got the correct speed on your putts.

Establishing the Basics

The Backward Chaining Method

When learning the game it is a good idea to start with a two-foot putt, and work your way backwards away from the hole so that you move from putting to chipping, to pitching to irons shots, and the last thing you would learn is driving. The advantage of learning golf this way is that players develop confidence and see success earlier as the tasks are easier to complete.

The putter should swing like a pendulum.

Golf can seem very complex, especially if you give a beginner a driver and ask him to hit 300 yards, as compared to trying to hole two-foot putts. But even complete beginners can achieve a good level of success if they start with a two-foot putt, and thereby begin to establish a base level of competence from which other skills can develop. This also gives players a feel for the game and will keep learners involved and challenged. This method is called the backward chaining method. The other advantage is that by learning putting first you are practising a big part of the game.

Making the Stroke

Many of the same ideas of the full swing apply to the putting stroke, as this stroke is essentially a mini swing; the main difference is that power is not an issue. In the putting stroke, short distances must be covered instead of having to cover a long way, so we make the stroke accordingly. As with the full swing, we have to establish a good set-up before being able to make the stroke correctly: if we don't, we will have to make compensations during the stroke, which makes it more complicated and harder to repeat.

Key Concept of the Putting Stroke

The key idea we are trying to produce in a putting stroke is to make the stroke like a pendulum – this is a great image to have, and you can try to recreate the tick-tock rhythm of a pendulum. A pendulum will take the same time to swing back and forth, within reason, irrespective of the length of the swing it takes, so it will have a consistent tick-tock or one-two rhythm. This idea is very important in how you control the length of your putts, and will be discussed later. Keep this image in mind when you are putting.

Different Styles and Techniques

The information given below will give you some fundamental ideas as to how to make a repeatable putting stroke. But watch a golf tournament on television, and you will undoubtedly notice that the players use a variety of techniques, grips, putters and putter lengths. All these different styles may have an element of the techniques described below – though ultimately, if the player gets the ball in the hole that is all that matters. Most good putters have the same key fundamentals in their putting stroke. Feel free to experiment with those methods and putters, but keep in mind the fundamentals described below because they will help make your stroke simple and give you some good foundations, and this is the basis of an effective stroke.

The Good Putting Set-up

Posture

The first element of a good putting set-up is good posture, where the aim is to stand in an athletic and balanced position. As with the full swing posture, aim to bend forwards from the waist and let your arms hang down in front of you.

Bend forwards from the waist to achieve the correct putting posture.

Ensure the eyes are over the ball, or just inside it.

Exercise to achieve the correct putting posture: Allow the putter to lean on your thigh, then let your hands hang down and bend forwards from the waist. Let your hands hang down in a natural position and clap them together. Ensure your arms are relaxed, and try not to think too much about where your hands should be. Now grip your putter, keeping your hands in that same position.

This exercise will help you achieve the correct hand position, which should be under the sternum; you should also feel your weight on the balls of your feet, and your eyes should be over the ball – note that they can be slightly to the inside of the ball, but never to the outside. This will allow the putter to swing on the correct path and the clubface to remain square to the path.

Aim

Aiming the putter face correctly can be more difficult than you would think, and quite a high percentage of golfers do this

incorrectly. This is largely due to the fact that you are standing to the side of the ball and are not looking directly down the target line. For instance, imagine if you were playing pool, and instead of looking directly down the cue you had to have your head to the side: this would make aiming the cue much more difficult. You have to train your eyes to recognize what the correct aim will be. You will need some feedback on what correct aim is, and the drills below will help you in this.

Aiming the Clubface
The most important element is to aim the clubface correctly. By aiming the clubface correctly at address, it will be simpler to return the club to a square position at impact. You can aim the clubface incorrectly and return it squarely, but this will require a compensation move during the stroke and this will lack consistency.

Drill: Use the line on the ball: Most golf balls have a line marked on them, or you

Aim the putter face at the target.

Use the line on the ball to help line up the face correctly.

can mark a line on the ball using a marker pen. Then stand behind the ball and line up the ball to your target using this line. On a straight putt this will be straight at the hole, while on a breaking putt it will be at break point. Once this is lined up correctly you can address the ball and align up the line on the ball to the line on the putter. You can also use this on the course: many professionals do this as part of their putting routine.

Drill: Putt along a chalk line: A builder's chalk line – available at most DIY stores – can help improve your putting. Draw a 10ft line with the chalk on a straight putt on the putting green, and then putt along this line. The chalk line and the line on your putter will give you a clear indication of where you are aiming. Also, see how well you can roll the ball along this line, which will give you a clear mental image of what you have to do to roll the ball into the hole.

Ask a partner to check your aim: Ask a friend to check your alignment. Tell them where you think you are aiming, and then get their feedback. Try this on a number of different putts and notice if there are any patterns to your aiming.

Aiming the Body
It is important to aim the putter face correctly, but aiming the body correctly will also assist good alignment of the putter face, and will send a stroke on the correct path. First, be sure your shoulders are parallel to the target line as this will influence how well you aim the putter face. Least important are the feet, as many established players have played equally well with both an open and a closed stance. For the sake of simplicity it is good to keep the feet parallel as well. However, it is quite all right to experiment with this, to find out what works best for you.

Drill: Put an alignment stick parallel to the chalk line: If you have your chalk line set-up you can put down an alignment stick parallel to it: this will provide a reference point for your body alignment.

An alignment stick parallel to your target line will help you line up your body correctly.

Grip

A number of different grips can be used. Watch a professional tournament and you will see that players use many different grips, and you can experiment with these to find the one that is most effective and comfortable for you.

Whichever grip you use, a common theme is that you must have a light grip pressure, as this will allow you to have a feel for the club head, and create a pendulum rhythm on your putter.

Two putter grips that you can try are the reverse overlapping grip and the cross-handed grip:

The reverse overlapping grip: This is the standard grip and one of the most popular, where the index finger of the left hand sits across the fingers of your right hand. This helps to keep your wrists out of the stroke so that you can make a pendulum stroke.

The cross-handed grip: This is a very popular grip where you turn your hands around so the left hand is below the right for the right-handed golfer. This has the benefit of making your shoulders level, and again helps keep the wrists out of the stroke.

Making the Stroke

We will cover some of the key elements of good putting and key fundamentals. These elements are noticeable in effective putters, even though they may have differing styles.

Making Good Contact

As with full shots, it is important to hit the ball out of the centre of the putter so that a consistent amount of energy is transferred to the ball. If you hit the ball out of the toe or the heel of the putter you won't transfer the correct amount of energy to the ball, meaning that your distance control will be inconsistent. Also your direction will be incorrect, as putts

The reverse overlapping grip.

The cross-handed grip.

hit on the heel will start to the left and putts hit on the toe will start to the right due to the clubface twisting when it is struck incorrectly.

Drill: Putt between two tees: On a 4ft putt put two tees in the ground just wider than the width of your putter. Then put a ball slightly in front of the tees and make some putts. To hit the ball out of the centre of the putter you will have to miss the tees on the forward stroke.

Putting through the tees drill to ensure good contact.

Path of the Stroke

The path of the putter will follow a slight arc, as illustrated in the diagram. It will start back fairly straight, then move on to an inward path, and then move back along the curve to impact. The club then starts to move gradually back along a curve to the inside, and will mirror that path off the backstroke. 'Inside' means inside the target line, which is the line we are trying to hit along. The clubface will remain square to this path.

By achieving this motion you will be more likely to return the clubface to square at impact, which will start the ball on the correct line. The amount of arc or curve on the stroke can vary from player to player. If the path becomes too much inside or outside of this curve it makes it more difficult to start the ball on the correct line. Keep this image in your mind when making the stroke.

The path of the putter.

Use Your Body Correctly

The Movement of the Shoulders

The putting stroke is focused on control rather than power, so the motion of the body is a lot quieter, and a mini version of the full swing. The motion is controlled by the slight turning of the shoulders, and works as a very small version of the full swing. The shoulders rock slightly back and forth, and this motion of the shoulders is the engine of the stroke. Keeping the upper arms connected to the body will allow the club to swing on the correct path.

Drill: Club across the chest and focusing on the left shoulder: Adopt your putting posture and put a club across your chest. Make a small turning motion backwards and forwards, and try to do this as you would in a full swing, but in a much smaller version.

Drill to get the left shoulder working correctly.

Drill to focus on the correct movement of the left shoulder.

Drill: Holding the left shoulder with the right hand: Take your stance, then put your right hand on your left shoulder. Then make some strokes one-handed, focusing on the movement of the left shoulder. The movement you are looking for is a slight turning motion, and you should feel the top of the left arm connected to your side.

The Lower Body
The lower body should be very still and quiet, as the bigger muscles of the legs don't need to work to create power. If the legs get too active it will discourage the putter working on the correct path and make it harder to make good contact. A good image to have for a stable lower body is to imagine that the legs are made

of stone and shouldn't move during the stroke. Or you can focus on your knees, because if these move, the rest of your lower body will move as well.

Drill: Super extra-wide stance: Address the putter and then make your stance as wide as you can: this will mean that you cannot move your legs and make some

A stable lower body.

An extra wide stance to feel a stable lower body.

strokes, and you will get a real sense of having a stable lower body. When you have done this a few times go back to a normal width of stance and you should have a more stable lower body.

Distance Control in Putting

Once you are making a good stroke it is important that you develop the skill of

The correct rhythm of the stroke is one-two, with one being on the backswing and two on the downswing.

This would be approximately a 10ft putt.

This would be approximately a 25ft putt.

This would be approximately a 50ft putt.

rhythm on all your strokes, but to change the length of swing to hit the ball different distances. The physics of a pendulum are that the time taken for a stroke will be the same, no matter what its length is. So the rhythm will be the same for a stroke, no matter what the length of the swing that you make in a one-two rhythm. The one is where you start your swing, and two when you start the downswing. By keeping the rhythm constant you will find it much easier to control the speed of your putts by changing the length of the stroke – the longer the distance to be covered, the longer the stroke. Also, taking the putter back and through the same distance will promote a pendulum rhythm.

The correct distance to take the putter back for each putt must be appropriate for the length of putt that is faced, and must take into account the speed and slope of the putt.

Common Mistakes

Same length of stroke but speed up the rhythm: If you make a short swing of the putter but have a long distance to cover the only way you can create enough force to get the ball to the hole is to speed up the stroke. This will create very inconsistent results and you will struggle to judge the distance.

Short backswing, long follow-through or long backswing, short follow-through: Both these mistakes will mean that you have to change the rhythm of the swing. When the backswing is too short you will have to speed up on the way through, and conversely when it is too long you will have to slow down. When you change the rhythm it becomes a lot harder to control the speed.

The Capture Speed of a Putt

The speed the ball should roll at is important, as the correct speed will maximize the size of the cup. This is referred to as the 'capture speed' or

controlling the distance of your putts. If the speed of the putt is good you will get the ball much closer to the hole, which, if you don't hole it, will make your next putt much easier.

Rhythm and length of stroke is key. Keep the image of a pendulum in your mind, as this is a great image to have of the stroke that we are trying to make. Alternatively think of the swings at the park. Notice that these have a one-two

rhythm, with one being counted on the backward movement and two on the forward movement. This pendulum motion is what we are trying to recreate in our putting strokes, and is something that many good putters have in their stroke. The stroke will be even on both sides of the ball, with the backswing being the same as the follow-through.

The key principle for controlling the distance of your putts is to have the same how far past the hole the ball would roll if it didn't go into the hole. The ideal speed for this would be 6 to 12in past the cup. As the ball is hit harder the effective width of the hole becomes smaller. So if you hit the ball harder you will have to hit the centre of the hole for it to go in, as opposed to putting at dead weight, where the effective width would be the entire hole. You should also consider the imperfections on the green: these will start to affect the roll of the ball as the speed slows, so there needs

Distance control in putting is instinctive, like throwing a ball.

Putt to the fringe, or in between two alignment sticks.

to be some speed on the putt to reduce this. By aiming to get the ball 6 to 12in past the hole you are balancing these two factors.

Make Distance Control Instinctive

Our aim is to make distance control in putting wholly instinctive, much as you would pitch and catch a ball. When we are playing 'catch' we don't think much about the technique or how far back we swing our arm, we just trust our instincts and throw. In reality we had a period of training on how to throw a ball, probably in our childhood, and that has developed into an innate skill. Much the same process needs to happen in putting, and although the proper technique of swinging the putter in a pendulum rhythm needs to be trained, our brain functions much

Place balls around the hole on different parts of the green and notice how they break.

better when we look at the target and react to it. The best way to make distance control instinctive is to practise the drill given here:

Drill: Putt to the fringe of the green: Take five balls and pick a point on the fringe of the green which you can either mark with a tee, or focus on in your mind's eye. Your aim is to roll each ball as close as you can to the fringe of the green. With this you will get feedback regarding how hard you have to hit the putt and make adjustments. Really notice how the ball rolls, the sounds and feel of the ball coming off the putter face, and how far away the ball finishes from the fringe. This will give you feedback about your distance control, and will help you learn to develop this skill. You will then make adjustments, and you will be surprised at how good you can become at rolling the ball the correct distance.

Reading the Greens

It is important that reading the greens comes after learning the mechanics of the stroke and the pace of the greens, because if you cannot start the ball on the correct line at the correct speed you will not get consistent readings on the green. You will notice that the speed at

Along the zero line the ball will roll straight and there is no break.

which you hit the ball affects the amount of break on a putt, where too much speed causes the ball to break less, and vice versa.

Drill: Around the clock focusing on break: Find a sloping piece of the putting green and put twelve balls evenly spaced around the hole, all about fifteen feet from the hole. By doing this you will have a lot of different types of putt. On each putt aim straight at the hole and notice what the break is on each putt, and how

the ball rolls. Don't try to play for the break or hole the putt: the aim is just to notice the break that is happening on each putt. Repeat this a few times and see if you notice any pattern: when were the putts straight? When were they right to left? When were they left to right?

Understanding Zero Lines
By doing the above drill you will have started to see the key principle in learning to read the greens. You will have noticed that when putting the ball directly up or

To the right of the zero line the ball will break right to left.

To the left of the zero line the ball will break left to right.

down the slope (along the 'zero line', as it is referred to) you had a straight putt, to the right of that the putts were right to left, and to the left the putts were left to right. This happens due to the effect of gravity and applies to any green that you will play. Once you have identified the zero line, understanding and working out the break becomes very predictable.

Games and Skills Tests to Improve your Putting

Luke Donald Drill: This drill will help you holing out short putts. You will need five balls and a tee. Place a tee 3ft from the hole and a ball next to it, and put the next four balls a foot apart in a line away from the hole. Then putt all the balls

FACTORS AFFECTING BREAK

Angle of the putt to the slope: This means where your putt is in relation to the zero line affecting your putt.

Slope: As the slope on the green changes, this affects the break. More slope will increase the break.

Speed of the green: The faster the greens are rolling, the more break there will be.

Distance from the hole: The further the ball is from the hole, the more the ball will break.

The information above has been gathered and developed by Aimpoint. These factors were first developed when Aimpoint started 3D modelling greens for television in the USA. From doing this they noticed that there were certain patterns to reading the greens that applied to whichever green they modelled, and they have developed a system from there. The great thing to know from this is that green reading is very predictable, as opposed to the old model of learning greens, which relied more on guesswork. For further information on Aimpoint contact your nearest certified instructor who will show you how to develop these skills further. Please see www.aimpoint.co.uk.

---

from the hole backwards. Repeat this four times. Keep track of your score out of twenty, and keep aiming to improve on your score each time. Your aim is to get fifteen or more. To make this more difficult, move to a hole that is on more of a slope so that you will have more break on the putts.

Around the clock: Place five balls around the hole a putter length away from the hole. Most standard putters are 35in, so this will leave you approximately 3ft putts. By having different putts around the hole you will have different angles of slope to deal with. Repeat this four times so you get a score out of twenty. Your aim is to get seventeen or more.

Putting par 18: On a putting green that preferably has nine holes cut on it, play the nine holes around the green and keep track of your score. If there are not nine holes, play each hole slightly differently. Each hole has a par of 2, and the green has holes of varying length and different slopes. Aim to get below twenty, and keep trying to achieve a personal best.

The Luke Donald skills test.

Around-the-clock skills test.

Putting par 18.

Birdie conversion test: Place three tees at five paces (12.5ft), six paces (15ft) and seven paces (17.5ft) away from the hole. This test will develop your ability to convert those birdie putts, as you are working on putts in the 10 to 20ft range. Putt ten balls from each tee peg and record your score. Your aim is to convert a third of your birdie putts on the course, so aim on this skills test to get ten or more.

Birdie conversion test.

CHAPTER 6

HOW TO CHIP AND PITCH

In this chapter the objectives discussed are as follows:

- Learn the next step of the short game
- Develop good fundamentals and the ability to apply good technique from short range and from bunkers
- Learn and play fun skills test to improve your skills

Your short game is a key area for you to improve, as chip and pitch shots will make up a large part of your game: statistically 70 per cent of your shots will be played from 100 yards and in. With 40 per cent being putts, that leaves 30 per cent of your game being chip and pitch shots, and this applies whether you are scoring around par or trying to break 100.

The first swing that you need to get good at is the basic chip of 15 yards: you will often encounter this shot on the course, and it is one that can have a big impact on your scores. When first learning you can start by using a pitching wedge, but you can use a number of different clubs with this same technique to produce a shot to work in each situation.

However, before working on different shots it is important to develop your basic technique. The basic chip should be simple, but many players really struggle with it, and becoming good at it can significantly improve your scores.

Basic Chipping and Pitching Set-up

As with the full swing, it is important that the basic set-up is correct. This will make the swing happen much more easily by making the correct impact happen more easily.

Ball position, width of stance, and going down the grip: The ball should be in the middle of the heel, as this is where the low point is. The stance should tend to be narrow, and narrower than it would be when taking a full shot. To have more control of the club you should make a shorter grip down on the club.

Your weight should favour the front foot: 60 per cent of your weight should favour the front leg, as this will also help to ensure that the low point of the swing happens in the correct spot.

60 per cent of your weight should be on your front foot.

Take up a narrow stance, with the ball in the middle of the heel.

Grip down the club for more control.

Keep your weight on your front foot as you swing.

Keep your weight on the front foot as you swing: During the swing your weight should remain in its starting position. This is because the power that would be created by the weight transfer is not needed on shorter shots. By keeping the weight favouring the front foot you will also ensure that the low point of the swing happens in the correct spot.

Keep the sternum moving through the shot: When playing the shot it is important that you keep moving through it. A key to focus on is that the sternum keeps turning and moving through the shot: if it stops,

Keep the sternum moving through the shot.

Keep the triangle of your arms.

Keep the arms soft, and maintain a good rhythm.

the hands will inevitably flip and break down, causing 'fat' and 'thin' shots. This is something you would naturally do when you throw a ball towards the target.

Keep the triangle: Much as on the full swing, it is important when playing a basic shot that the triangle shape of the arms is kept. This will ensure that a flat left wrist is maintained at impact.

Keep the arms soft and a good rhythm: It important that you keep the arms soft while playing this shot so that you can get a good feel for the distance, as tension will reduce the amount of feel you have for the shot. The rhythm of the swing should be a smooth, swinging motion much like a pendulum.

Drills

Hit off on your front leg to keep your weight forward: Address a chip shot as normal, then put your back foot on its toe: like this you will be forced to keep your weight on your front leg both at address and during the swing. As you do this, also make sure you keep your sternum moving.

Hold the finish and check that your left arm and club make a straight line: Your finish position will give a good indication of how well you have made the swing. At the end of the chip swing the hands should finish just in front of the hips. If you take your right hand off the club, your left arm and the club should be in one line. If the left wrist has become bent, you won't have this straight line relationship.

Keep the sternum moving: Take your address position and then put your left hand on your sternum. Now make some swings, and focus on keeping your sternum moving through the shot: by having your hand there it will give you a good awareness of keeping it moving through.

Hit off on your front leg to keep your weight forward.

Hold the finish and then check to see if the club and your arm are in one line.

The wrists flipping and the triangle breaking down.

Keep your left hand on your sternum: like this you will know you are keeping it moving through the shot.

Common Mistakes

The triangle breaking down and the wrists flipping: Much as on the full swing, flipping of the wrists can be caused by the instinct to try and scoop the ball in the air. This causes fat and thin shots, and makes it very difficult to make consistent contact.

Keeping the head down: This may seem the opposite to what your golfing companions have been telling you for years, but when you focus too much on keeping the head down, the sternum stops moving through and often the weight will remain on the back foot; then the triangle will break down, with the

Keeping the head down causes the sternum to stop moving through and the wrists to flip.

wrists flipping as above. This will cause the low point of the swing to move backwards, which will cause 'fat' and 'thin' shots.

Hitting at the ball instead of swinging: Often when something above is not correct it will cause a miss-hit, and in an attempt to make good contact the natural reaction is for a player to speed up and make a jerky motion through the shot that hits the ball. This will make distance control and correct contact difficult and inconsistent.

Hitting the Ball to a Landing Spot

Once you have developed a good technique, the basic skill of chipping is to hit the ball to a landing spot – that is, to a point that will let it run out to your target.

Hitting a good landing spot is the key to good chipping.

Practise chipping to a circle.

Much as if you were going to aim a ball at a target, you are unlikely to try and land the ball straight into the hole: instead you will try and land your ball on a spot or in a zone that you have judged suitably close to the target, depending on the distance to the target and the ground conditions, plus the trajectory and the speed with which you intend to throw the ball.

This is something we all do instinctively, without much conscious thought. What we are trying to do in a chip shot is the same thing, except we are trying to do this with a club and ball. You may have seen footage of Rory McIlroy on television when he was young, chipping balls into a washing machine. He was very good at this, and what that developed for him was the skill of hitting a ball to his landing spot. In fact, hitting the ball to a spot on the green must have become very easy for him if he could land it in the washing machine. So when he got on the golf course all he had to do was learn how to pick his landing spot, depending on the conditions he was faced with. As chipping is such an important part of the game, you can see that this skill contributed to him being able to save a lot of shots.

Drill: Chipping to a circle: Make a circular target that is 6ft in diameter and place it 10yd away. The target can either be a target circle or you can use a piece of rope. Take ten balls and see how many you can land in the circle, and then record your score. I would recommend using your pitching wedge, but you can try with different clubs. How did you do? Was this more difficult than you thought?

Deciding the Best Landing Spot

Once you have become proficient at landing your ball on a landing spot, what you then have to get good at is deciding the best landing spot for each shot that you play. There are many different factors that will affect this, and you will not always get it right, but it is important that you practise and develop this skill. Be aware of the factors below that will affect where you judge your landing spot to be. There is no exact science that will give you the perfect landing spot every time, as there are many different factors to account for, but keep the following guidelines in mind, and through practice you will develop the skill of judging where this landing spot is.

Distance from the hole: The distance from the hole will affect where you have to land the ball. The further you are from the hole, the more spin you will be able to put on the ball.

Lie: Different lies will affect the amount of spin on the ball: for instance, if there is grass between the ball and the club this will affect the amount of roll on the ball. Generally the worse the lie, the more the ball will roll.

Elevation: If you are above the landing spot you will get a softer bounce and the ball will run less. If you are below the level of the landing spot the ball will run more.

The firmness of the green or landing area: The firmer the green, the more the ball will bounce, and vice versa.

The club: The club you are using will affect the trajectory and spin on the ball, so if you don't have much green to work with you may want to use a more lofted club, and if you have a lot of green use a less lofted club.

Which Club to Use for Chipping?

There are two different schools of thought when it comes to what club to use when chipping: either you can vary the club you use, or you can use the same club. The advantage of using the same club on each shot is that you will be able to get used to how that club reacts and performs, which should enable you to get the ball closer to the hole. The disadvantage is that you won't have much variety in the shots you will be able to play easily. You can

You can use different clubs with the same technique to produce a variety of shots.

either add loft, which will hit the ball higher, or de-loft, for a lower shot, but this can be more difficult to perform consistently.

Alternatively you can vary the club to fit the type of shot that you have, using more loft when you have less green, and less loft when you have more green to work with. This is a good guideline to have when you are starting to understand which club will suit you. Try several different shots around the practice green, and use a sand wedge, a pitching wedge, a 9 iron and a 7 iron to work out which club works best for you in each situation. Vary the length of shots you have, and the amount of green that you have to work with.

More Good Ideas

Land on the green if you can: You can't always land the ball on the green but try to if you can, because you will get a more predictable first bounce. If you land the ball in the rough the first bounce will always be less predictable.

Try to land on a flat spot: Again, this will give you a more consistent first bounce. If you land the ball on a downslope it will tend to shoot forwards, and vice versa if you land it on the upslope. This won't always be possible but will allow you to get the most consistent first bounce.

Look from the side for a better view: When working out where your landing spot might be, try to get a side view of the area because you will get a better perspective of the shot you are facing. You can do this as you are walking to the shot. You will find that the task will look different from the side than it will from behind the ball, and you will be able to make a better decision from the side. Look for where you want to land the ball,

Look from the side to get a better view, and decide on your landing spot.

8 o'clock swing.

9 o'clock swing.

11 o'clock swing.

Wedge	8 o'clock	9 o'clock	11 o'clock
PW			
Gap wedge			
Lob/sand wedge			

Work out how far you carry each wedge with each length of swing and record.

and visualize where you see the ball landing and how it will run.

How to Pitch

Pitching is much the same as chipping, but the basic difference is that a pitch spends more time in the air than on the ground, as opposed to a chip which spends more time on the ground. The technique is very similar to the chip shot, in that the same fundamentals apply.

Controlling the Distance

The key to good pitching is distance control. Most people will not be too far left or right of the target, but will be either too far from or too short of the target. Once you are making a good stroke and contact with the shot, the key concept that controls the swing is the same as the putting stroke. *The distance is controlled by the length of the swing: the rhythm stays the same.* This will give you consistency, and the distance you hit with your wedges will become very predictable.

Using the Clock
The key fundamental to controlling the distance of your wedges is to understand the varying lengths of backswing required for each distance. Imagine your left arm is the hour hand on a clock, and different times give you different distances. Use just three to start off with, and these will provide you with a good base. Begin with 8 o'clock, 9 o'clock and 11 o'clock, or half swing, three-quarter swing and full swing.

Look at the pictures on the previous page and practise getting the correct length of backswing. You can use a mirror or video to give you some good feedback on how well you are doing. It is a good idea to do this with all your wedges, and to record each distance. Write this down in your yardage book, or by putting a sticker on the back of your wedges.

Use a Range Finder
A range finder will help you get better at distance control with your wedges. When practising on the range this will give accurate information about your targets, and you can work out what length backswing will hit the ball a certain distance. Plus, it will give you good information on the course to help your distance control. If you don't have a range finder you can use a yardage book, or pace out yardages; this will also help you with your three different distances with each wedge. But a range finder will make this much easier and more accurate.

Have a Good Wedge Set-up
Have a good set of wedges with the correct loft progression, because the wedge set-up you have in your set will greatly help your distance control. The loft of the club is the angle of the club in respect to the shaft. You can have the loft checked by most PGA professionals, and what you want is an even spacing of the lofts so that you will get a good spacing of the distance you hit each wedge. The spacing should be

Use a range finder to get accurate distances.

approximately 5 or 6 degrees between each wedge. Common set-ups would be 47, 52 and 58 degrees or 48, 54 and 60 degrees. Be aware of this if you are buying new wedges.

How to Practise

If you go to the range, work out how far away the targets are. Try to practise at a facility that has a good number of targets inside 100 yards, and work on going to each target. Alternatively, if you have a facility where you can hit your own practice balls, mark out three targets that are at three different distances, such as 20, 40 and 60 yards, and hit shots to them. You can use alignment sticks or an old shaft as your target. In each instance work out what length or swing is required to hit the ball the correct distance. Ensure you hold your finish, and keep getting lots of good feedback.

Playing from Bunkers

Bunkers are designed to be a hazard and are a source of much frustration for many golfers. They require a different shot to other parts of the game, but if you understand a few simple concepts they are in some ways a simple shot. What happens to many players is that by not understanding the simple ideas described below, going into a bunker can wreck their score by either leaving the ball in the bunker, or by thinning the shot through the green. If you apply some of the ideas given below you can reach your first goal of getting out of the bunker and on to the green. Add in some practice and you could start to get your bunker shots up and down.

- **Hit the sand and not the ball**
  When playing a bunker shot you want to play it like an explosion shot, where you hit the sand and not the ball. You want to hit the sand 1 to 4in behind the ball, which as long as you use the bounce of the wedge correctly means you have a margin of error on this shot, unlike shots from the fairway. A great image for you to have is that the

Get your wedge set-up correct with an even spacing of lofts.

Imagine the ball sitting in the middle of a £10 note.

ABOVE: Increase the bounce by opening the clubface.

Open the wedge first, then take your grip.

ball is sitting in the middle of a £10 note and you want to enter the sand at the back of the note and leave at the end. If you do not take any sand this would be too little, and vice versa.

- **Use the bounce of the wedge**
  If you look at the bottom of your sand wedge you will notice that the back edge of the club is lower than the front edge. This is the bounce, and it is designed to do exactly what it says: hit the ground and then bounce so that the club does not dig into the ground. This will be your best friend in the sand, and will make a big difference to your performance in the bunkers. The amount of bounce that the club has in a square position is not enough for bunker shots, so increase the amount of bounce by opening the sand wedge so that the club will point to the right of the target. Notice how much the bounce angle has increased.

Open the wedge first and then take your grip: it is important that you open the club first and then grip the club, as opposed to taking your grip and then opening the club.

Get your sternum behind the ball.

Make twice the swing that you would make on a normal shot of the same distance.

Keep turning through to your finish.

above the 1 to 4in zone where you want to hit the sand behind the ball.

- **Hit the shot harder**
  As you are hitting the sand and adding loft to the club you will have to make a longer swing than you would for a shot for the same distance from the grass. A good guideline is to make a swing twice as long in the bunker as you would for a normal shot; on a standard bunker shot this will be an L to L swing.

- **Hit the sand and keep turning through the shot to your finish**
  Once you have set up to the shot correctly you have completed the most vital part of the stroke. During the stroke, aim to hit the sand and keep moving through the shot to a good finish position. At the finish your sternum should be facing the target with your weight on your left side and you arms extended into an 'L' position. This is the same as with a pitch shot.

Listen to the sound that your shot makes: If you perform the shot correctly you will make a distinctive 'thud' sound when you make contact; this will give an indication of how well you have used the bounce, and will give you great feedback. Notice the sound you make, and see if you can hear the difference between a good shot and a bad shot.

Look at the divot you have made in the sand: Look especially where the divot started, as this will give you great feedback as well. If you didn't take enough sand and hit too close to the ball, you will hit a thin shot. If you hit the sand too early or the divot was too deep, you will hit a fat shot. You are looking for a divot like the £10 note that was discussed earlier.

- **Get good at the basic bunker shot**
  Most bunker shots that you have will be greenside bunker shots, which are 15 to 20 yards from the flag. Focus your time on getting proficient at this shot to begin with, and then work on playing longer bunker shots and bad

- **Driver-width stance and dig your feet into the sand**
  Take a driver-width stance with your club, as this will help lower the bottom of the arc of your swing so that you ensure you hit the sand before the ball. Then dig your feet into the sand, which will also make sure that you hit the sand and not the ball. Digging your feet in will also enable you to test the texture of the sand to get a feel for the shot that you are about to play.

- **Get your sternum behind the ball**
  The bottom of the arc of your swing will be where your sternum is, so to ensure again that you hit the sand and not the ball, you want your sternum

lie bunker shots later. The tougher shots are less frequent.

- **Playing from different types of sand and lies**
  The same technique will be effective for different types of sand and textures of sand. Bunkers at courses vary greatly in the type of sand they have and the amount of sand in the bunkers. The above technique will work in firmer sand, with the only adjustment being to go slightly closer to the ball, as opposed to very soft sand where you would aim slightly further behind the ball. But these are just minor adjustments, and the bounce of the sand wedge will help you play all shots in different lies.

- **Practise this shot often, and it will help your long game**
  You will become more competent at this shot by practising it regularly. If you have had difficulty in playing this shot in the past, be patient while implementing the above techniques into your game. Also, becoming competent from a bunker will help your long game, because you won't be apprehensive about going into a bunker. The mindset that you need when playing to a green that is surrounded by bunkers is that if you go into a bunker you can play from them competently. If you are nervous about going into a bunker this will add tension to your full shot swing, and invariably increases the likelihood of the ball going into the bunker.

Most bunker shots will be 15 to 20 yards, so practise these the most.

By becoming competent at bunker shots you won't be nervous of them, which will help your long game.

PART 3

MORE ADVANCED SKILLS FOR INTERMEDIATE AND ADVANCED PLAYERS

CHAPTER 7

DEVELOPING THE SWING

In this chapter the objectives discussed are as follows:

- Learn more advanced swing ideas for intermediate and advanced players
- Develop the full swing with a good body motion and swinging the club on plane
- Understand the correct impact position

In the last section on the swing we discussed how to set up to the ball in order to start to develop the swing by making good contact with a mini swing and a three-quarter swing. Once you have developed these techniques, and if this is being performed correctly, you should be making good consistent contact with the ball. The swing should start to become more natural and more instinctive without you having to consciously think about it as much any more. It is important that the fundamentals are retained and monitored, but the aim is now to develop the swing further. In this section the aim is to provide aspects to work on, so that you take your swing to a more advanced level technically.

The Full Swing

The Finish Position

The finish position is a great indicator as to what has happened in the swing – you might not think that the finish had any effect on the outcome of your shot. But when you hit a great shot you end up in a balanced position watching the ball and admiring your good work, so a good finish is a good position to focus on because it indicates that you have created good positions through the shot.

RIGHT: Good balance is essential.

BELOW: Back foot on its toe and hips facing the target.

The Key Aspects of the Finish Position

Weight on the front foot and facing the target: Indicators that your weight has transferred through the shot and your body has pivoted correctly through the shot are that the back foot finishes up on the toe and the hips face the target. You should also be looking at the target.

In balance: Good balance is important for a good swing as it will enable you to make a consistent contact. Finishing in balance will also show that you have the correct rhythm and balance in your swing.

Continue the 'L' position with the arms extended away from the body.

Keeping your head down often results in a poor finish position.

Arms extended away from the body: If you have maintained the correct extension and release through the shot – you have maintained the triangle and L positions described in Chapter 3 – the arms should be extended away from you with the elbows fairly close together.

Common Mistakes

Keeping the head down for too long: The age-old tip of keeping your head down often causes more problems than it solves. Keeping your head down for too long and overfocusing on this causes the weight to stay back and the triangle to break down. It also moves the low point of the arc backwards, which means that good contact is difficult.

Arms collapsed with the elbows far apart: When a person swings the club across the ball as a way of compensating for the poor path of the club, they keep the clubface open by the elbows working apart and the left arm working very high. Alternatively the triangle through the shot breaks down, and the arms end the swing very close to the body; this move will cause you to slice.

The Body Turn

The correct body motion is the engine of the golf swing: it is what powers the golf swing, and by using the body correctly you will be utilising the big muscles of the body to create power. Also, the correct body actions will allow the club and arms to work correctly, whereas poor body action means that you will have to make corrections. If the body works correctly the arms and club will follow. The turning motion is very similar to how you would throw a ball a long way: you make a dynamic move by turning your shoulders, loading your back leg on the backward

The arms have collapsed and not extended away through the shot.

The correct body turn is very much like a throwing motion.

motion, then you rotate and move forwards with the body to face your intended target. Your arms follow the motion that the body makes. Keep this in mind when you are working on your body motion.

Movement of the Shoulders and Hips

On the backswing the shoulders should turn approximately 90 degrees so that your back faces the target. They can turn slightly more but not too much, as this will not give you much more benefit and can lead to too long a swing. The hips should turn as well to approximately 45 degrees, with the right hip turning backwards. This turning motion should be a dynamic move, and a great image to keep in mind is that you are coiling like a spring ready to make an explosive move through the shot. On the through-swing there should be a slight lateral move of the hips to the target, and then the motion on the backswing is mirrored

where the hips and shoulders turn through to face the target.

Movement in the Downswing

Start the downswing from the ground upwards: At the start of the downswing the move starts from the feet, then the knees, hips and torso follow. This is the

proper sequence in the downswing, which allows the club to work on the proper plane – much like a throwing motion where the first move of the forward motion starts with a step to the target, this is a key move in applying maximum power to the ball. A simpler way to think of this move is to start the downswing with a bump of the left hip towards the target. This is only a subtle move where

The shoulders turn back to 90 degrees and the hips turn to 45 degrees.

The downswing starts from the ground upwards.

The feet remain stable and the right foot rolls off the toe.

the hip moves no more than to the outside of your left foot, and you should only focus on this move in the first half of the downswing.

How the feet move: The feet are there to stabilize the swing. The left foot should remain fairly stable in the backswing and downswing, and should not leave the ground. By staying stable like this you will have good balance during the swing, which will increase the likelihood of making good contact. The left foot leaving the ground on the through-swing may increase your ability to create power, but unless you are a player who works hard at the game and has great athletic ability you will achieve greater consistency by keeping the left foot planted.

The right foot is key to creating power in the downswing. In the backswing it stays stable and weight is loaded into the right heel; on the downswing it holds position until halfway into the downswing. From there the right heel starts to rise and you start pushing off the inside of the right toe. The foot will roll towards the target and continue to come up on to the right toe. The right foot is how you can uncoil that spring that you loaded in the backswing.

Common Mistakes

Swivelling on the right foot makes it harder for you to transfer your weight to

The right foot swivelling on the way through.

your front foot in the downswing. It can also cause you to swing the club across the ball, and will result in poor sequencing of the swing. It also makes the through-swing ungraceful and much more difficult than it should be.

Movement of the Head

During the swing it is important to keep the head *steady* because if it moves too much it will move the low point of the swing arc. Be aware that it should be a

The head remains steady throughout the swing.

steady head, but not a still head: the head can move slightly both backwards and forwards and up and down, but it should not move excessively. On the backswing most players' heads will move slightly to the right, and halfway through the follow-through the head will move up and forwards slightly. The head can also move down slightly, as this will encourage you to hit down on the ball.

Drills

Arms across the chest: This is the best way to train the correct body movement in the swing. Place a club across your chest and cross your arms. Then get into your address position as if you were going to hit a ball. Now turn your shoulders to rehearse the backswing position. Make the move very slowly and really focus on one element of the turn that you need to improve. Try to copy the move in the pictures below. Once you are confident you are making the backswing correctly, move on to making the downswing motion. Again, practise this slowly until you can make the move correctly, then make the whole move without stopping. Practise this in front of a mirror to receive some feedback. This is an easy drill to perform at home.

Step drill: This drill will help you to start the downswing from the ground up. Take your address position with a club, and bring both feet together. Then make your backswing and stop at the top. At the top of the backswing the first move you make is a step with your left foot forwards, and then swing through to your finish. It is important that the step is the correct width: it should be to where it would be for a normal shot or back to shoulder width. Again, do this slowly to begin with, and stop at the top of the backswing before starting the step. As you improve you can increase the speed, and even hit balls doing this drill.

The 'arms across the chest' drill to train the correct body movement.

Step drill to start the downswing from the ground upwards.

Understanding Swing Plane

The swing plane is the angle at which the club swings in relation to the ground. There are many different ideas on what the correct swing plane is, but it is important because it allows you to create the correct swing path so the low point of the swing happens in the correct place: this will make controlling the clubface much easier. Below are some ideas and checkpoints that should help you to understand the swing plane.

Establish the Parallels

One of the easiest ways to check and understand if your swing is on the correct plane is to make sure the club is working parallel to the target line. The target line is a line drawn from the ball to the target – though first we have to establish that our body is parallel to the target line at set-up by lining up correctly. An 'on plane' swing will have the club shaft parallel to the target line four times during the swing. These parallel positions are common in some of the best players in the world.

Parallel One: Halfway Back
By getting the first takeaway position

Parallel one: halfway back.

correct you will make it easier to get the other positions correct, and will make getting the rest of them much more likely. If this is incorrect you will have to make a compensation somewhere in the swing to get the club back to a good delivery position, or parallel number three. The club head here should be in front of the hands, and the club should be just over a line across your toes. If the club head is inside the hands, as is very common, the club is too much inside and on a flat plane, and the shaft will point to the right of the target. If the club head is outside the hands the club head will be to the right of the hands and the shaft will be pointing to the left of the target.

Parallel two: top of the swing.

Parallel Two: Top of the Backswing
This is usually a continuation of a good position in the first parallel: with this correct you will be set up to make a downswing, and will not have to make any compensations. The club should be over the right shoulder, and the length of the swing should be parallel to the ground. If the club goes back too far it will cause the parallel to point to the right. If the club shaft points to the right of the target it will be across the line and if it points to the left it will be laid off.

Parallel three: halfway in the downswing.

Parallel Three: Halfway in the Downswing
This is the most important parallel because it indicates that the delivery position of the club is correct and the club is on the correct path. The other parallel positions can be compensated for in the swing, but if this isn't correct it is unlikely you will be able to correct it at this late stage of the swing. By getting the first two parallels correct you will increase the likelihood that this will be correct. This position should be similar to parallel one. If the club head is to the left of the hands this indicates an inside position, which will mean the path is too far from the inside. And vice versa if the club head is to the right of the hands, which indicates the path will be too much to the inside.

Parallel Four: Halfway through the Follow-through
If both parallels three and four are correct, this indicates that the path of the club is correct. If the club shaft is pointing to the right of the target this shows that the path is too much inside, and if it points too far to the left the path has been too far from the outside. Although the ball has already gone, this parallel is very much an indication of what has gone before, and often by getting this parallel correct you will improve previous parallels, especially parallel three.

Parallel four: halfway in the through-swing.

Drill – Rehearse Parallels One and Four

Make practice swings working on one and four. Do this slowly and remember this is only a half swing. You could use a mirror to give you feedback and get these positions correct so that you train them to become automatic. You can then hit some short shots with a short iron, again

focusing on getting both these parallels correct.

Get the Shaft Pointing to the Ball

Another good idea on checking if you are on plane is where the shaft is pointing in relation to the target line. The key checkpoint here is when the club is in the L position, or three-quarters back. If you draw a line from the shaft back to the ball it should be pointing at the target line, or halfway between the feet and the target line. If it points outside the target line the club will be too flat, and if it points too close to the feet it will be too upright. The same idea should be seen on the downswing where the shaft should point directly at the target line when the club is in the three-quarter down position.

Leverage and Lag

Imagine trying to throw the ball as far as you can without using your wrists. If you simulate a throwing motion you will find it

At halfway back the shaft should be pointing at the target line.

very natural to cock your wrist as you move backwards and then release the wrists through the shot. The cocking and uncocking motion is a source of power, and by utilizing this in the golf swing you will add power and accuracy to your shots, plus it will allow you to control the low point of the swing. The use of your wrists is called the leverage of your swing, and you should think of the wrists working in three different stages.

Set the leverage in the backswing: Setting the wrists the correct amount in the backswing is where they are first loaded. When you are working on the L swing you are achieving this because you are creating a 90-degree angle between the left arm and the club. This will continue to the top of the backswing, where the angle should still be 90 degrees – though this angle can be slightly different, with a tolerance of 10 degrees either way.

Rehearse parallels one and four.

In a throwing motion the wrists are a source of power.

Set the wrists correctly by establishing the L position.

Hold in the first move of the downswing: In the first move in the downswing the energy needs to be stored where the wrists retain their angle or lag. This angle should remain at least at 90 degrees when the left arm is again parallel to the ground, but it is all right to increase that angle, as many players do, because this move allows you to increase the amount of energy stored. It is good to focus on keeping the angle in the right wrist. Also, the right arm, and specifically the right elbow, will have to remain soft in the downswing to keep the lag in the downswing.

Hold the lag into the first move of the downswing.

Keep hold of the lag into the last part of the downswing.

Keep the lag long into the downswing: If you were going to lose the lag it would generally be in the first move of the downswing. Once you have kept it during the first part of the downswing you must keep it well into the downswing until just before impact.

Release the stored energy: As when you are throwing a ball, the energy you have stored in the wrists must be released. So the angle retained in the right wrist must be let go as the club reaches its maximum speed through the hitting area. Once the right wrist is released, the right arm will rotate over the left arm in the hitting area.

Common Mistakes

Losing the lag and casting from the top: One of the most common swing faults is losing the lag in the downswing, which causes weak and mishit shots. This often comes from trying to lift or scoop the ball into the air, and not understanding that you need to make a downward strike. When this happens, focus on the right wrist in the downswing and on retaining that angle during the downswing. Plus, rehearse the following drills.

Drills

Pump drill: Go to the top of the backswing and hold. Then practise the first half of the downswing by pumping the club down to the halfway position, focusing on retaining the angle in the right wrist. Practise this move three times by returning the club from halfway down to the top of the backswing position, and then make your swing to the follow-through. This will help you focus on the first part of the downswing.

Split hand drill: At set-up, split your hands apart on the grip, make a normal backswing, and hold at the top of the swing. With the hands being apart you will feel easier if the right wrist is losing its angle in the downswing. Then practise making downswings back to the ball – as

Release the stored energy into the ball and past it.

The pump drill, to hold the lag in the downswing.

the right arm is further away from the target it is easier to feel the lag retained in the downswing.

Swoosh drill: This drill is to work on the release, which is the last part of why you retain good leverage. Take a wood and turn it upside down, and hold the club by the head, ensuring that you hold the grip 6in off the ground and that you don't strike the ground with the grip. Work on

swinging the club as quickly as you can, and making a loud swoosh with the club through the hitting area. As the club held this way is very light it will be easier to move it quickly, and the louder the swoosh, the more club-head speed you are creating. You will have to really let the club go, and work on trying to create as much speed as you can. This will help train you to increase the club-head speed and hit the ball further.

The split hand drill, to maintain the lag.

The swoosh drill, to develop club-head speed.

Striking the ball out of the centre of the club.

The Correct Impact

The aim of everything that we have discussed so far is to create the correct impact position. The ball will do what it is told to do at impact, so if we want to control what the ball does, we have to create the correct impact condition. The aim of everything else that we have done is to make impact easier and likely to happen more often. The elements of a good impact described below are verifiable and present in all good golfers.

Centred strike: Striking the ball in the centre of the club is something all good players do consistently. Every player has hit that sweet strike which feels correct and makes a great sound. Good contact also comes before distance and accuracy, because if you don't make the correct contact you won't hit the ball as far as you could. This is often seen at driving ranges, where there are often many players making maximum effort, but not hitting the ball out of the centre of the club, which results in erratic shots that don't go very far. This is also why learning the mini swing is a great way to start to develop the skill of striking the ball.

Flat left wrist: By having a flat left wrist at impact you are applying a downward strike and pressure to the ball. This is called 'an imperative' in Homer Kelley's book *The Golfing Machine*. If the left wrist is breaking down, this signifies a scooping

A flat left wrist at impact.

motion. By developing and then keeping the triangle swing discussed earlier you are working on keeping the left wrist firm, and developing this.

Weight forward: The weight must be forward at impact otherwise the low point of the swing will be moved back. By moving forwards through the shot you will be using the bigger muscles and the mass of your body to apply the hit to the ball. This can be developed by working on the mini swing, and focusing on moving the right knee forwards, through the shot. Also, by working on the correct full swing finish you are getting the weight to move towards the target in the swing.

Controlling the low point: The club moves on an arc, and we want to the hit the ball at the bottom of that arc, if not slightly before. By having a consistent low point you will make good contact more often. The flat left wrist, the weight forward, and the path of the club all have an influence on the low point because if these are incorrect the low point will be moved. You will also notice how good the better players are at hitting the same point of the ground with their swings.

The weight forward at impact.

Controlling the low point.

This is partly good mechanics, and there is also a skill element that has been developed through thousands of repetitions. This is something that you need to develop, because there are very few other sports where the ball is on the ground as it is in golf.

The path of the club: This is the path the club comes into the ball. A great image to have of the correct path is a curve. The correct path is from inside, to square, to inside the target line. By getting the path correct you will be more likely to deliver a square clubface to the ball.

The club path moves on a curve into the ball.

The club path moves on a curve into the ball.

The clubface controls 85 per cent of the direction of the ball.

Clubface control: The most important factor in controlling the start and curve on the ball is the clubface, since the clubface angle is 85 per cent of the controlling factor in determining the starting direction and the curvature of the ball. Getting the clubface square will mean that you will hit straighter shots, which start and end up at your target more often.

Club-head speed: This is the speed with which the club head moves through the shot, and assuming the other impact factors are correct, greater club-head speed will hit the ball further. Hitting the ball further doesn't guarantee lower scores, but you do need a certain level of club-head speed so that you can reach par 4s in two shots – and it is an advantage.

Club-head speed creates more distance.

CHAPTER 8

EFFECTIVE PRACTICE

The following objectives are discussed in this chapter:

- To understand how to make the most efficient use of your practice time
- To understand the different types of practice and how we learn
- To make practice fun and challenging so that improved performance is seen on the course

Many golfers don't make the most of their practice time, and fail to understand why they can't take their improvements on the driving range on to the golf course. The reason for this may be that much of time, how you practise is nothing like the way you play on the course. If you go to the range and hit a bucket of balls at the same target with the same few clubs, this is nothing like you would do on the course. You will rarely hit the same club two times in a row, let alone fifty times as you might do on the range. The answer is first, to understand that there are different types of practice, and then to introduce practice that is more like what you will face on the course. This is important for all levels of player.

The Stages of Learning

The first thing to understand when you are learning a new skill is that you will go through different stages of learning as you do so, whether it is the game of golf as a whole, a specific move in the swing, or developing your mental skills. Whatever you are aiming to improve, you should understand that you will go through the following stages on your road to mastery:

- *Unconsciously incompetent:* You are not aware that you do not have the skill to carry out a task or see the usefulness of acquiring the skill
- *Consciously incompetent:* You become aware of your lack of skill to carry out a task
- *Consciously competent:* You are working on developing the skills to carry out a task, but this requires seriously conscious focus to perform it
- *Unconsciously competent:* You can perform the skill necessary to carry out a task instinctively and without conscious thought; the skill becomes second nature

If you think of any skill you have developed you have probably gone through this same process. A good example is learning to drive a car. When you first started to learn you had to think deliberately of setting the accelerator, putting the clutch down, releasing the hand brake – but I am sure that now you just get into the car and perform all these actions without much thought and can do them instinctively. This is the stage you want to attain in developing your golf skills, but to get to it will take several hours of deliberate practice.

Deliberate Practice

To develop your skills requires you to practise with a clear purpose and a clear idea of what you are trying to achieve. Jack Nicklaus said that it was important to practise with a purpose, and that if you were just smacking balls you were getting exercise and not practice. If you had watched Jack practise you would have seen that he gave every shot the same focus that he would have done had it been the last hole of a major championship. In Daniel Coyle's *The*

Talent Code he looks in depth at this idea. When you are practising deliberately you are focused and get lost in the task at hand. You may lose track of time, which may pass quickly, and you will learn from your mistakes by making adjustments.

By performing several hours of deliberate practice you will produce a physical change to the brain. Coyle states:

Each human movement, thought or feeling is a precisely timed electric signal travelling through a chain of neurons – a circuit of nerve fibres. Myelin is the insulation that wraps these nerve fibres and increases signal strength and accuracy. The more we fire that circuit, the more myelin optimizes that circuit, and the stronger, faster and more fluent our movements and thoughts become.

So the more deliberately we practise, the more we are actually physically changing our brains to work better and faster by making the neural circuit work better and produce more myelin. In top performers the neural circuit for their required skills is very efficient, and the myelin has been produced to make this happen quickly through many hours of practice.

Steps for Deliberate Practice

Before you begin on a plan of improvement it is important to understand the current status of your game, and this will vary greatly depending on your prevailing level of play, your experience, and the amount of time you have already invested in your game. If you are a beginner your first objectives will be to learn the fundamentals of each part of the game, and to learn to make good contact. If you are an advanced player your objectives may be more complicated: you will want to look at all areas of the game including your technique, short game, clubs, golf fitness, mental game, practice habits and lifestyle factors. Each player should investigate this as much as possible, and it is important to take good advice about this from a PGA professional and/or a professional who specializes in a certain area. This advice should be tailored to yourself and to your current level.

Assess your Current Game

Using some basic statistics about your game can highlight which areas are strengths and which are weaknesses. What you are looking to develop is evidence on what you are good at, and what you need to work on. Much as a business must produce accounts to demonstrate its performance, if you can have some basic numbers on your golf game you will better understand where you need to improve, and over time you will be able to track your improvement.

When you decide to embrace statistics will depend on the level of your game. If you are a beginner you may only want to after a period of playing, and maybe start with just putts per round. Even if you are a pro or advanced player you can go overboard on statistics, but you should have a good understanding of your game. You will also find that in certain areas you may be better than you thought, and that in others you are not as good as you thought.

The basic key stats you should look at are these:

- Fairways hit – the number of fairways you hit per round
- Greens in regulation – the number of greens you hit in regulation per round: for a par 3 this is in one shot, par 4 in two and par 5 in three shots
- Putts per round – the number of putts you take per round
- Up and down – the number of times

per round when you miss a green and get the ball into the hole in two shots
- Sand saves – the number of times you get down in two shots from a greenside bunker
- Scoring average – what your average score is

In later sections I will go through this in more depth, but for now if you have these basic stats, which should be recorded over a minimum of five rounds, you will get some evidence about which areas of your game need the most attention to be able to make a plan of improvement. These stats could be recorded on paper, a spreadsheet, or on one of the numerous statistical software packages available today. Make a note of which areas you are good at, and which need the most attention.

Outline Your Plan of Improvement

Once you have assessed your current standard of play, you should identify some clear steps you can take to improve your game. You can then prioritize these and work on each step. For example, you may have a lesson and identify with your coach that a certain swing move is causing you to miss fairways and not hit as many greens as you would need. So you identify a plan to improve your technique, and to better understand why you hit good shots and poor shots.

Another course of action could be that you have a lesson on the aspect of the game you struggle with the most, such as putting, because you are having a high number of putts per round. Many people don't have lessons on the short game. Or you could focus your practice time on a weak area: instead of always going to the driving range you could spend half of your time on the putting green instead.

Other aspects of your plan that you might wish to look at include questions such as whether your golf clubs are the correct fit for you? Or, do you manage your game around the course well and make good decisions based on your ability? Do you have a good attitude? Are

you golf fit? You will have some good ideas on these parts of the game in upcoming sections, and they are just as important as technique in improving your overall performance on the course. Use the 'tick list' below as a way to start developing your plan, according to whether the area is a strength, or could be improved:

- Technique
- Putting
- Chipping/pitching
- Bunkers
- Course management
- Use of practice time
- Mental game/attitude
- Equipment

Exercise: Three Actions to Improve your Golf

Write down three actions that you need to take, and can take immediately, to improve your golf; this may be from booking a lesson to changing how you spend your practice time. Now is always a good time to start improving. It is important that you write these actions down, and once you have achieved them you can move on to the next three. If you have more than three actions you can write them all down, but identify which are the current priorities.

Use Your Time Effectively

Each of us has only limited practice time, and it is important that we use it effectively. The demands of modern life means that we are pulled in many different directions, and if we want to improve our golf we must use our time well.

Decide how much time you can devote to golf each month, then break it down into how much you can practise each week. Most people with a busy lifestyle could commit two to four hours a week to practising, as well as the number of times they can play. Out of a week of 168 hours this represents a very small part. Nevertheless, by having a clear plan and using these few hours effectively you can achieve a lot and make some substantial improvements – even better if you can commit more time. But remember, even if you had all week to practise, you must still have a plan of how you will use your time – just because you put in many more hours of practice, there is no guarantee that you will improve if you are not focusing on the correct things.

Make Each Shot Count

Make sure you are correctly focused on each shot, and take your time: each shot must be given equal attention, and remember quality is more important than quantity. Aim to be like Jack Nicklaus and play every shot as if it were on the last hole. Remember what your goals are for the session, and what you are trying to achieve. Maybe take a break and sit down to think things through – and enjoy the good shots.

Types of Practice

Generally speaking there are four types of practice:

- *Technical:* Where you work on a particular move in the swing or short game, and are focused on improving the movement to produce better shots
- *Game:* Playing games and challenges to test your skills and abilities with measurable results
- *Skill:* Developing different skills that will help you have better control of the ball
- *Rehearsing:* Preparing for different situations and for events in the future

Technical Practice

Technical practice involves working on a specific move in your swing. This requires a lot of correct repetitions in order to establish a specific move, and will require more effort when you first start working on it; however, it should become easier over time. A guideline could be that when you go to the driving range you spend your first forty balls working on this move – or you may want to spend time at home

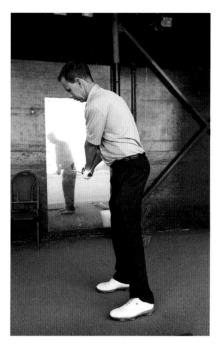

Concentrate on one move at a time when working on your swing.

practising the move using a mirror to give you feedback (here I am working on my takeaway). Working without a ball in front of a mirror is a great way to work on a swing change, because you have immediate feedback about what you are doing.

Work on one thing at a time: It is important that you work on one move at a time – if you try to work on two or more moves in the swing you will only think too much, and risk becoming confused and losing focus. In *The Talent Code* Daniel Coyle states: 'In talent hotbeds participants look at the task as a whole, secondly they divide it into its smallest possible chunks'. In other words, take one step at a time, and only move on to the next step once you have mastered the current task.

Make the movement in slow motion: When aiming to train in a new skill it is important to perform the skill slowly. In martial arts many complicated techniques

are performed in slow motion to begin with, in order to achieve a good technique, and only then speeded up to the point where they can be used in actual fighting. In golf, when working on a new move in the swing, make a swing at half the speed you would normally use while focusing on the particular area you are working on. This will allow you plenty of feedback as to how the correct move should feel, as well as enabling you to train the move you are trying to achieve. This technique was used by Ben Hogan and by the great Harvey Penick when working with his students.

Hold a position: Identify this position and hold it for 30 seconds. Initially this will be difficult, but it will allow you plenty of feedback as to what this position that you are trying to achieve, feels like. You will train the position, and you will also start to recognize when you do and don't achieve it.

To train a move, hold the position you are aiming to achieve for 30 seconds.

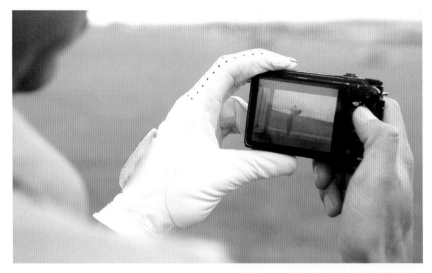

Videoing your swing will give you great feedback.

Using video – seeing is believing: A great tool when you are working on your swing is to use video, because 'seeing is believing'. Often what you feel you are doing and what you are actually doing is very different, and you may be surprised at what you are actually doing. You will also receive some very good feedback, which is a key to improving. Ensure that you have a clear understanding as to what you are looking for, be careful not to over-analyse, and remember to look at one thing at a time.

Vary your targets

Moving On

The amount of time you spend on technical practice will vary. When you first make a swing change this may occupy 80 per cent of your practice time, but as this improves you could spend less time working on technique and move into other types of practice. However, even if your technique becomes very good, you are happy with your shots, and the results are happening, you may want to spend a small amount of each session checking the key technical points of the swing. You may want to check this in a mirror at home, or spend the first fifteen balls of the session working on this. It will also be worth having a lesson to check, and to use a video camera to see how well you are doing.

Game Practice

Another type of practice is where you try to recreate how you would normally play in a game, and thereby challenge your skills. The aim of this kind of practice is to play more like you would on the course where you are not having too many technical thoughts, and you are focusing more on the shot at hand and your target. Here are some ideas about how you can do that.

Hit to different targets: When you are on the range, try changing targets on each shot. Many people only hit where the mat is pointing them. But on the course, what happens is that you get lazy and aim where the line of the tee aims you. But often this points where you don't want to go, causing you to hit into trouble.

Change clubs at each shot: Just as when you are playing, try changing clubs on each shot. On the range you could play an imaginary round, or even simulate a hole that you have problems with, so you will be more confident next time you are in that situation.

Change clubs at each shot.

Set a goal and aim to hit your tee shots through that goal.

Hit through the goal: Set up a goal on the range and aim to hit your ball in between the goal markers. This goal should be between 30 and 10 yards wide, depending on your ability. At first, aim your ball to start through the goal, and as you improve, have the ball finish in the goal. You can also reduce the size of the goal. This drill will help you get better at hitting the fairways. Give yourself ten balls and record how many you get through the goal.

On the chipping green play par 18: In this exercise you play nine holes around the chipping green, with each hole being a par 2. You will need only one ball and you will have a score to demonstrate how well you played. This will give you a good indication as to how good your short game is, and you will start to get into the habit of getting up and down. Try to give yourself three easy shots, three medium and three hard shots. This is a great game to play against a friend.

On the course play best ball or even worst ball: Be sure that the course is quiet: this is a great exercise to do by yourself. You play nine holes, and on each shot play two balls, and in best ball choose the best shot. Then play two balls on each shot until you hole out. So if you play a bad shot or make a wrong decision you will be able to learn from it and make an adjustment, which you don't get the opportunity to do during normal play. If you hit a great shot you don't have to hit another. But it will help to develop your confidence, and as you get better you may find you don't need to hit the second ball as much.

Keep track of your score doing this. More advanced players can make practice harder than the real game by playing the game of worst ball, where you hit two shots each time but have to play the worst one each time. This is difficult and will require you to focus on each shot. You will find next time you play normally it seems a lot easier, and you will learn to make the best score you can.

Playing par 18.

Playing best ball or worst ball.

Skill Practice

Skill practice is about developing the skills to play golf and your ability to perform tasks. The skill will develop by learning to perform the task. This approach is much like being thrown into a pool and being asked to swim when you haven't before – you will learn how to swim rather than being taught how to swim. Of course it is to be hoped that you would be given some pointers or that the pool is shallow! The ability to perform these tasks also develops technical ability. Even once you have developed a technically sound swing there is also skill required, and this needs to be developed as well. These are skills that many good players can perform, so when learning them have fun with them – and don't expect to perform them perfectly straight away, but aim for steady improvement.

Practising keepy-ups.

Keepy-ups: Much like football where players can keep the ball in the air, this is golf's version and is great for developing hand-to-eye coordination and feel for the ball. Start by holding the club halfway down, then drop the ball but try to keep it from falling to the ground by letting it bounce on the club. See how many you can perform, and keep trying to beat your personal best. As you improve, work your hold on the club shaft back until you are holding it on the grip to perform the keepy-ups.

Balance Drills

Balance is a key requirement to play well; it is evident when a balanced finish position can be maintained. The sense of proprioception is where the body senses movement and aims to keep it in balance, and this sense can be developed. The drills described below will challenge your balance by narrowing your base of support, but will thereby help to improve it.

Feet together drill: Take your normal set-up with a 7 iron, and then bring your feet together so that your heels are an inch apart. Now take some swings at an easy pace, and work on hitting the shots in balance. If you lose your balance you will learn

Hitting with your feet together.

Hitting off one leg.

from the feedback; keep hitting shots until you can finish in balance. This is a great drill for good balance and rhythm, and you will be surprised how far you can hit the shot with very little effort. After ten shots go back to hitting shots with a normal stance, and recreate the feeling.

Hit off one leg: Take up your normal stance, then move your back foot back and raise your heel so that only your toe is touching the ground. Then hit shots at three-quarter pace. Notice if you can swing in balance, because it will be more difficult, and keep hitting shots until you can. Again, after ten shots hit some shots with a normal stance and become aware of your balance. Do you notice anything different?

Hit shots with no shoes on: By taking off your shoes you become more aware of your balance, and get some great feedback as to how good it is.

The great Sam Snead often practised this drill to develop good balance and rhythm in his swing. As you hit shots you will learn where your weight is balanced both at address and through the swing. At set-up, aim to ensure that you can feel that your weight is

evenly spread on your feet, and that you are really connected to the ground. Pay attention to your balance during the swing, and in particular aim to finish in good balance. After twenty shots put your shoes back on, and again notice what feels different.

Hitting with no shoes on to improve balance.

One-Armed Drills

One-armed drills require a considerable amount of strength and good technique to perform correctly. The idea of doing these is that if you can perform a one-armed swing correctly, then hitting with two arms should be easy. One-armed swings are easy to do poorly, so it is very important that if you are going to do them, you do so with good technique, otherwise you will get no benefit from them, and may even harm your development. Only use a 9 iron to start with, and if you are hitting shots, make sure you hit off a tee. Also, only hit ten shots per session with each arm so that you don't stress it unduly, and overdo

things, at least until you have done the drill over several sessions. These drills are hard work, so aim to get gradually better over time at them. ('Left arm' and 'right arm' are correct for a right-handed golfer; if you are left-handed this will be the other way round.)

Right arm only: Take your normal address, and then put the back of your left hand just below your right elbow: like this you will be able to get the right elbow in the correct position, and it will encourage you to turn your shoulders properly. Aim to get your right arm into a throwing position, just as you would when you throw a ball a long way with your shoulders turned. The right arm should

make an L shape, and you should aim to mimic the accompanying pictures. First make a number of practice swings doing this, and ensure that you can do it with the proper technique. Once you feel comfortable doing this, then you can hit some shots.

Left arm only: Take your normal stance, then put your right hand behind your back. For most people the left arm will be their weaker arm. Aim to turn your shoulders properly, also to get your left thumb under the shaft when you are at the top of your swing, and with the arm extended as well. On the way through let your left arm fold. Again, aim to mimic the accompanying pictures.

Right arm only drill.

Left arm only drill.

Shaping Shots

When making your ball curve intentionally the technique is very similar to how you would make the ball curve in other sports, such as a free kick in football. If you were right-footed you would come more inside the ball, aiming to get your foot around it to make it spin from right to left in the air. Or if you were playing tennis and you were to slice a forehand shot, this would be similar to a fade or a slice, as opposed to a topspin shot which would be like a draw or hook shot.

This is a great way to start to understand how to shape your shots. To begin with take a 7 iron and hit half shots

Hit the draw by closing the clubface through the shot.

with the aim of getting the ball to curve with a smaller swing, before hitting fuller shots. Also, if you take an alignment stick and place it 10 yards in front of you, this will give you a target to aim for and curve the ball around.

Hitting the draw: Aim to the right of your stick, where you would like the ball to start. Then as you go through the ball, release your hands more quickly than normal to close the face through the shot – the feeling should be similar to when you make the topspin forehand shot. Notice how the ball flies, because it will give you direct feedback as to how well you did. Did it start to the right of the stick and move to the left in the air? If it started too far left you closed the clubface too quickly, and overdid it with the release through the shot. If it started to the right of the stick and it stayed straight you may not have used enough hand through the shot. Experiment until you get the correct amount, and use each shot as feedback as to how you are doing.

Hitting the fade: Aim to the left of the stick where you would like the ball to start, then do the opposite of what you were doing on the draw shot and hold off

your release through the shot – much as if you were trying to hit a tennis slice shot. This will open the clubface and make it curve to the right. Again, notice where the ball starts, and if it curves in the air. If you overdo it the ball may start to the right of the target and curve to the right too much. If you don't do it enough, the ball may stay straight. Keep getting feedback from the ball flight and making adjustments to how you release the club through the shot.

Rehearsing

The difference between practising and rehearsing is that in rehearsing you are trying to recreate the situations that you will be facing in the future, and you are preparing yourself to deal with these situations. If you have prepared for a situation you will be calmer and more likely to be able to deal with it effectively when you are faced with it. Below are some different ways you could rehearse.

Rehearse on the practice area: Imagine yourself in situations you may find yourself in on the course at your upcoming round or tournament. Visualize the situation

with the club you may need, give yourself an appropriate target, and do what you can to recreate different circumstances you are likely to face. This may be a particular drive or iron shot, or situation – such as being tied for the lead coming down to the last hole. This can also be done on the practice green, such as making a 10ft putt on the last to achieve your target. Also, you can work on any problem shots you have been dealing with.

Mental rehearsal and playing 'What if': You don't always have to be at the course to work on your game: you can do a lot at home by visualizing or imagining what you would like to happen. Find a quiet place where you won't be disturbed and can relax: there you can run through the situations that you are likely to face, and see yourself dealing with them successfully. Don't always assume that every situation will go to plan, because invariably it won't. You want to be able to deal with many different situations, and to be prepared, so ask yourself what you would do in certain situations, such as, for example, double bogeying the first hole: how will you respond? Or what if you birdie the first four holes? How will you

feel, and how will you conduct yourself? Also, prepare yourself for playing with different playing partners and formats. Use past experiences, and learn from how you dealt with them in the past, and decide what you would do in the future.

Hit the fade by keeping the clubface open through the shot.

Rehearse on the course: When you are playing practice rounds, or when the course is quiet, you can put yourself in different situations on the course that you are likely to face, or work on shots that you may have problems with, so that when it comes to the actual round you will have faced that situation already. Give yourself difficult shots, and evaluate where you might miss a shot. Try some tough shots and ones that you have had trouble with in the past – though be careful not to upset the greenkeepers by playing numerous balls, but just play one or two shots from these situations. Look for spots where you may have a shot, depending on your tendencies. Many people have a hole they have problems with, so go on the course and find a solution by trying a different approach or club off the tee.

In Conclusion

Using the above practice ideas will allow you to make the most of your time: it is important that you work on your game in the most effective way possible so as to speed up your improvement and thereby maximize your enjoyment of the game.

Rehearsing on the range to prepare for upcoming situations you will have to deal with.

CHAPTER 9

FITNESS FOR GOLF

The following objectives are discussed in this chapter:

- To make the connection as to how physical limitations affect your swing and are the root cause of swing faults
- To demonstrate physical tests you can perform to assess your golf fitness
- To demonstrate easy-to-perform exercises to correct any physical limitations

It is important to be fit for golf because it is your body which is going to swing the club. The key connection that you need to make is that you can only do what your body will let you, and if you work on your fitness you will be able to make improvements in your golf. Often when you make an improvement in your fitness you will see an improvement in your swing.

Improving Flexibility

When talking about fitness you may imagine a routine of getting up early and running several miles, or of lifting heavy weights. But the first and most important element of fitness that will help your golf improve is flexibility. Any physical limitation will affect your golf swing, and no matter how much you practise you will find it very difficult to make improvements in your technique.

The level of flexibility that you need is not extreme, but through testing numerous tour players and top amateurs the Titleist Performance Institute (mytpi. com) and others have found that a number of minimum flexibility requirements are needed to optimize your golf swing. If a player's physical weaknesses can be identified it will be

possible to determine how these limitations inhibit their swing, and then a programme to correct these limitations can be prescribed.

The best way to assess flexibility is to have a screening with a qualified fitness professional. They will give you a number of different tests – between ten and thirty – for different areas related to flexibility and stability, as well as some strength tests to determine a player's physical strengths and weaknesses. These tests will not be overly difficult, but from this assessment corrective exercises can be prescribed.

When starting a new fitness programme you should always consult your doctor and follow their advice. If you do not have access to a fitness professional, the tests described below can be performed yourself.

Once you have completed a screening the fitness professional should discuss with your coach the relationship between what your body can physically perform and your swing faults. A player can then take a two-way approach to improving their swing, by improving their physical capabilities through corrective exercises, and working on the range with their coach to improve their game. This will be more likely to see improved performance, with a lot less frustration and in a much more efficient way. So if you have been struggling to make improvements to your swing in the past and have not seen much success, this may be the reason why.

Test your Golf Fitness

Below are six easy-to-perform basic fitness tests that will help assess your physical condition and indicate whether there is a physical limitation preventing

you from making your best swing. This is not an exhaustive list of tests: the aim is to help you assess your golf fitness so that you can then follow it up with appropriate fitness exercises. It is advisable to perform all the tests slowly, and to stop if you feel any physical pain while performing them. Some of the exercises given are corrective, and it is important that you perform these with a good technique. Aim to perform each stretch three times, holding for 30 seconds. There are also several exercises to improve each area. Please consult a fitness professional before beginning an exercise programme.

The Hamstrings

What these muscles are, and why they are important: The hamstrings are the muscles in the back of the legs, and they are important because they work to maintain good posture in the swing.

The hamstring toe touch test: From a straight standing position with your feet approximately 6in apart, bend forwards from the waist keeping your legs straight. Keep going as far as you can without bending your knees. This should be easy, but many people struggle to complete this.

A good result: You should be able to touch your toes. If you cannot, this may indicate tight hamstrings.

The hamstring sit and reach test: Sit with your upper body upright and your legs straight out in front of you. Hold a club in the fist of your hands, and stretch forwards moving the club towards your toes. Stop when you have

Toe touch test.

Sit and reach test.

Raised foot stretch.

the test, then stretch forwards as far as you can while keeping your legs straight and hold for 20 seconds. Aim to increase the stretch on each repetition, and repeat the stretch three times.

Turning your Upper Body Past your Lower Body

What these muscles are, and why they are important: In the golf swing the shoulders turn through 90 degrees at the top of the backswing as compared to the hips, which only turn 45 degrees. It is important that you can turn your shoulders past your hips to make an effective shoulder turn as the body turn is the key source of power and accuracy in the golf swing. If you have a limitation in this exercise you may find it difficult to make a shoulder turn in the backswing and the through swing.

gone as far as you can or your legs begin to bend. Also, keep the club in your fist and don't let it slip down to the fingers.

A good result: Ideally you should be able to get the club to your toes. If the club is 6in back or further, this will indicate tight hamstrings.

Corrective Exercises
Raised foot on a chair: This is a simple exercise and excellent for people with very tight hamstrings. Lift your left leg up on to a chair, keeping it straight, then with the left hand stretch down the leg as far as you can go, being sure to keep the leg straight all the while. Feel the stretch in the back of the leg and aim to go slightly further each time you do the stretch. Repeat on the other leg. Do three repetitions on each leg, holding for 30 seconds.

Sit and reach: The test we performed above can also be the stretch. Get into the same sitting position as you did for

Sit and reach stretch.

The test: Sit on the front of a chair with your legs out straight and in a 90-degree position. Take a club and put it across your chest with your arms folded, and now turn your shoulders backwards and forwards as you would in a golf swing – by sitting in a chair you will not be able to move your lower body. Notice how far you can turn both to the right and to the left to see if this is the same both ways: it is quite common that this is more difficult one way compared to the other.

A good result: The outcome you are looking for is being able to turn your shoulders 45 degrees in both directions.

Testing your ability to turn past your lower body.

Open book stretch.

Corrective Exercise
Open books: Lie on your side with your legs bent and your arms out in front of you. Keeping your legs touching, try to rotate your upper body all the way across your body, keeping your arms at the same level as your chest and aiming to get your arm to touch the ground. Perform this on both sides.

90/90 shoulder stretch.

Shoulder Flexibility

What these muscles are, and why they are important: Mobility in the shoulder joint will allow you to have good extension, and will also help you maintain your triangle and L positions in the swing.

The 90/90 shoulder test: While standing upright, hold your right arm by your side at 90 degrees; bend your elbow so that it is at 90 degrees as shown. Then raise your hand upwards by rotating your shoulder while maintaining your upright posture. Stop when you can't move your shoulder any further. Repeat this exercise on both shoulders.

A good result: To pass this test you should be able to get your arm up to 90 degrees on both sides: if you cannot, this will indicate that you have some tightness in your shoulders. Ensure you keep your posture, and stop when you feel tightness because you are not aiming to force the joint back.

Corrective Exercise
Reach, roll and lift: First, kneel down on the ground and sit back on your heels as in a prayer position. Place both arms up on a Swiss ball or a chair, then reach out your right arm as far as possible over the ball keeping your trunk stable. Roll your palm to the sky, and then try to lift your

arm up off the ball or chair. Make sure you only lift your arm, and not your trunk. Repeat this on both sides.

Lats Flexibility

What these muscles are, and why they are important: Your *latissimus dorsi* ('lats') muscle is the larger muscle on your back and the back of your arms. This muscle is important to allow you to extend your arms and rotate them properly.

The test: Lift your left arm and put it down your back over your left shoulder, then put your right arm behind your waist

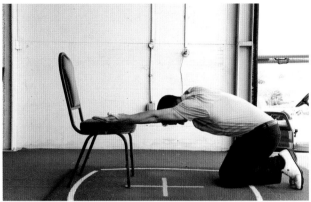

Reach, roll and lift stretch.

and up your back, as shown in the photo. Aim to get your hands as close together as you can so that you can touch your fingers. Repeat this with your arms the other way around.

A good result: You should be able to stretch enough so that the fingers of your two hands meet, whichever way round you do the exercise. If you can't, this will indicate tightness in your lats and upper body. Notice as well if you find this test easier on one side compared to the other, because often one side will be tighter.

Lats flexibility test.

Prayer stretch.

Prayer stretch on a club.

Corrective Exercises

Prayer stretch: Start in a kneeling position and place your arms on a Swiss ball or a chair; then roll the ball or push the chair slowly away from you. Keep going until you feel a big stretch in your lats – but stop if there is any pain.

Prayer stretch on a club: Take a 5 iron and put the club out in front of you with both hands on top of the grip. Then bending forwards from the waist, stretch your arms and the club out in front of you until your spine is parallel to the ground. Hold this stretch for 30 seconds.

The Ability to Deep Squat

What these muscles are, and why they are important: The deep squat tests flexibility in your hips, ankles and knees. Tightness and inflexibility in these muscles will make it very difficult for a player to perform the deep squat properly, and this means it is very difficult to keep the posture in the golf swing and may cause the spine angle to move up and down, which will cause inconsistent shots.

The test: Standing in an upright position, cross your hands across your chest and then squat downwards. Stop if you feel any discomfort, if your heels come off the ground, or if you lose your balance. This should be performed slowly so you are always in control.

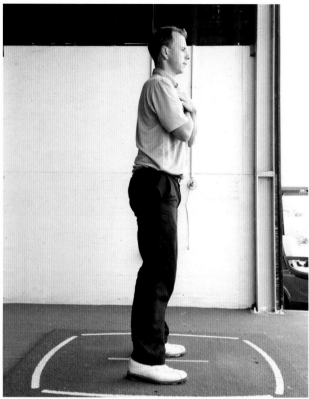

Deep squat test.

Deep squat with arm stretch.

A good result: You should be able to squat downwards keeping your spine upright, with both heels on the ground while keeping your balance and in a controlled way.

Corrective Exercise
Deep squat with arm stretch: Stand on something that you can put under your heels, such as a broom handle. Squat down and extend your arms upwards, then slowly stand up. Be sure to do this slowly, and only do eight to ten repetitions of this exercise.

Test your balance by standing on one leg.

Balance

What these muscles are, and why they are important: Balance is a key skill of any athletic movement. Your weight in the swing is being transferred into your back foot in the backswing, and then forward to your front foot in the through swing at speed. It is important that you remain in balance to make correct contact and to complete the swing athletically.

The test: Stand on one leg, and once you are balanced, close your eyes. Hold this position as long as you can: the test stops when your foot moves or you lose your balance. Repeat the test on the other leg.

A good result: If you can hold your balance on each leg for 30 seconds this would be a good result. You may be better on one leg than the other.

Corrective Exercise
Single leg balance: Simply stand on one leg and hold your balance, at first with your eyes open and then with them shut. To make this harder, lift your heel off the ground.

Single leg balance by standing on one leg and lifting your heel to make it harder.

CHAPTER 10

EFFECTIVE MENTAL APPROACH AND COURSE MANAGEMENT

The following objectives are discussed in this chapter:

- To understand some easy-to-implement mental strategies to improve performance
- How to review your game using some basic statistics
- To understand key guidelines for good course management

A good mental approach is an essential part of good golf and of getting the most out of your game, and as the level of your game improves the more important it will become. A good mental game will not be overly important until you have become competent at the fundamentals of the game – if you have bad technique on shots no amount of happy thoughts will overcome this. But once you have become competent and are starting to develop you can introduce some of these basics of the mental game: they will get you through all the situations that you will face on the course and give you the best chance of hitting good shots.

The two things you have to control are the ball and yourself (*Golf is Not a Game of Perfect*, Rotella), so developing your mental skills can have a huge impact on your performance on the course. These skills can be developed just like physical skills, and they are just as important because your game develops in physical competence. You don't have to understand the detailed workings of the mind to have a good mental game, and I would recommend further research if you would like to understand them in more detail. Below are some simple-to-implement techniques that are used by

some of the game's best players, and if you work them into your game they will help you to perform at your best.

Picking Targets

You have to be focused on where you want the ball to go. This is the nature of sport, and if you are not focused on the target then you are more than likely focused on something negative, such as the out of bounds or mis-hitting the shot. Your target should be as specific as possible so your mind has something very small to focus on. This is a similar idea to other sports such as, say, football, where for example David Beckham will aim for a

specific part of the goal when he is taking a free kick, or Roger Federer will aim for a specific spot in the tennis court. You will not always hit your target, but by having a narrow focus you will have more chance of doing so.

You will also discover that by being focused on your target your bad shots should not be as bad. Furthermore, if you do the opposite, that is, of not focusing on your target, and of thinking of everything else but where you want the ball to go, you will be in a very negative state and much less likely to hit the ball where you want it to go.

Pick an elevated target: A good way to help you focus on where you want the

Pick out a specific elevated target.

Put your bag slightly back and to the right.

ball to go is to pick an elevated target such as the top of a tree. This will help, because when you look at a low level target the last thing you may see before you swing is trouble. By picking a higher target you won't see the trouble so readily, and will be able to make a more positive swing.

The smaller the target the better: Better players will pick as small a target as possible: thus instead of aiming for a tree, they will try aiming for a specific branch of the tree in the distance. You may not always hit that target, but that is how our mind works best. This is how we have evolved over time, and it may go back to our caveman days when hunters had to spear an animal in the heart or head to ensure their dinner was caught. What you don't want to hear is that a player is aiming rather vaguely down the fairway somewhere – what we do want to hear is that he is aiming at as small a target as possible.

Pre-Shot Routines

A good pre-shot routine will allow you to develop consistent habits and is the foundation of playing consistently. It will enable you to set up consistently to the shot so that you can take the correct grip and aim on each swing, and – even more important – it will help you focus your mind on the shot at hand. If you watch a professional event you will notice how consistent good players are with their routines, and they will perform this routine almost identically on each shot they hit. You may also notice that when this routine varies they hit a poor shot. It will become your best friend in pressure situations and enable you to establish good habits without having to consciously think of them. Each player's routine will have variations, but all with the same aim, of getting the player completely focused on the shot at hand.

Where you put your bag is important: If you get into the habit of putting your bag down slightly to the back and to the right of your ball, you will be in a position to decide how you want to play the shot, and to take into account all the different factors that you need to play a successful shot. You will also be in a good position to stand behind the ball and look down the target line.

Start behind the ball and make your decision about how you want to play the shot: Most good routines start behind the ball, and from this position you are looking directly down the target line. This means you are in a good position to decide on how to play the shot, because you can account for the factors which will affect how you play it, such as lie, wind, distance and so on, so that you can make a decision on your target and shot selection.

Visualize the shot: Once you have made the decision about the shot you are going to play, then you can visualize the shot you want to hit, and see it going to your

ABOVE: Start behind the shot to decide how to play it.

BELOW: Visualize the path of the shot.

target. Different people will visualize in different ways: some will see the ball's flight and the ball travelling across an imaginary line to the target; others will just see the target and the ball going to it. Individual variations are fine, but the aim is to see your ball going to where you want it to go, so that you have a positive image in your mind about how you want to play the shot. This image will also help your unconscious mind to produce a swing to make the ball go to your target.

Make rehearsal swings: A better way to think of your practice swings before you hit a shot is that they are rehearsal swings. This swing should be made to recreate the swing that you want to make, instead of just swinging the club. The number of swings that you make is up to you, and you may not even make a swing at all. But if you do, try to make it as close as possible to the swing you want to make.

Commit to the shot and let it go: Once you have gone through this process, the last part of a good routine is to commit to your shot and let go of the result. You want to make a positive swing to your target without worrying about the result.

Post-Shot Routine

After you have hit your shot it is important that you have a post-shot routine so that you can approach the next shot in a good frame of mind and learn as much as you can from each shot. Although the shot you have hit has gone, how you react to it can affect the following shot – for instance, getting angry about a bad shot can cause a run of bad shots.

10 yard rule: Imagine there is a line 10 yards after the shot. By the time you have reached that line you should have got rid of any anger that you have about a bad shot. You can get as angry as you want before that line, but after that you have to let it go and move on so that you don't carry any anger to the following shot, causing agitation to build. This may not be easy at first, but keep working on this technique. Breathe deeply to help calm yourself, and ensure you have a positive body language.

Use your practice swing to rehearse the shot you want to play.

Aim to let all your negative emotions go by the time you have gone 10 yards past your last shot.

Get excited about your good shots and keep neutral about your bad shots: Golfers can be very hard on themselves and often forget to enjoy their good shots, but you should take time to enjoy them. Take in everything that these shots give you, such as the feel of the strike and the sight of your ball going to your intended target. Ben Hogan said he only expected to hit one or two perfect shots in the round, and he is regarded as one of the best ball strikers of all time, so be sure to manage your own expectations because you will not hit every shot as you would like. With your bad shots aim to be neutral about the result, and attach no emotion whatsoever to such

a shot. This will be a daily struggle and will often take time to develop, but as you get better at this you will remember more of your good shots.

Positive Body Language

Think of someone who is depressed and you will often see their state of mind in their body language before they say anything. Their head will be down and their step will be heavy, which will indicate they are in a very negative state. A negative attitude and head down is something that you don't see in golfers who are playing well. When a sports person is playing well they have a

confident body language, and you can see they are in a positive state.

We can affect our state of mind by taking control of our body language, and by making our body language positive we can put ourselves into a more positive state. In fact psychologists have found a direct link between body language and a person's mental state, so by changing your body language you can change your state. This is particularly important when you are having a bad run of holes, because if you can take control of your body language you can improve your mental state and turn round a bad run of holes.

Keep your head and eyes up throughout the round: Next time you play, aim to

Get excited about your good shots.

keep your eyes and head up for as much of the round as possible. Walk positively, and become aware of when you enter a negative state of mind. To address this negative state, immediately walk taller with your eyes up, and you will be aware of an improved attitude, which will help you play better.

Trusting Your Swing

Golf is a game of trust and faith, and the whole purpose of practising, taking lessons and buying equipment is to allow you to make a swing that you trust, and which will hit the ball at your target. You can't make the ball go where you would like it to go: you have to make a swing where you let go of the result and just focus on your target. This means making the swing a less conscious movement on the course, and moving to a subconscious athletic movement where you are focused on your target. This is something that good players do when they are playing well: they simply pick out a target, see the shot they want to hit, and hit it. This is difficult to do when you are playing badly, but you will perform better by trusting your swing even if it is not performing for you on that day.

The aim of practising is to think less, not more: An important principle to remember as you practise is to make your swing and game instinctive and full of good habits that support you playing your best. As you develop the habits you are training, you will become subconsciously more competent: this is what each player is aiming for, and why good players practise so hard.

Focus on your target and don't think about swing mechanics while you are playing: When on the course forget worrying about your swing technique, such as your swing plane and how your wrists work, but just focus on your target. Worrying will over-involve the left side of your brain, and this will impair your natural athletic ability. The

Keep your eyes up and take control of your body language.

place to improve your mechanics is on the driving range, so when you are on the course let go of this and just play.

Remember your good shots: To build confidence in your ability to play well you must have a good memory of your successes and good shots. The more you can vividly remember your good shots, the more you programme your mind to reproduce those shots on a subconscious level. Confidence is

developed through having good references of performing the task successfully in the past, so to become confident we need to build numerous references. Through practice and from your playing experience, if you remember your successes you are building confidence. The alternative is to remember your failures and constantly feed yourself with references of how you performed badly, which makes it very difficult to build confidence.

Talk about the good in your game: Often golfers can be heard telling everybody in detail about their bad shots, but by doing this they are just programming themselves for more bad shots, as they are developing an in-depth memory of them. Instead, talk about and remember your good shots, because this will develop positive memories, which will develop confidence. Harvey Penick once told Tom Kite when he first went out to play the tour to always have dinner with good putters because they will talk positively about their putting.

Remember your three best shots from each round: Sports psychologist Karl Morris prescribes that after each round you write down in detail your three best shots. This will develop your memory of your good shots, and when you have a similar shot you will have a reference of being able to produce a good shot in the past.

Acceptance

The last characteristic of a good mental approach is acceptance of the outcome of your shots and the game. You have to accept whatever shot you have played, and go and play the next shot to the best of your ability. This shows that you have a degree of detachment from the result, and that you can play the next shot to the best of your ability.

Accept the nature of the game: The game of golf is very difficult and is often not fair. You will get bad bounces, and some days whatever you do, things will not go the way you want. If you accept the nature of the game you will deal with the inevitable ups and downs much better. No one has yet perfected the game and everyone hits bad shots, but what each player aims to achieve is to

improve and reduce the number of bad shots.

Accept the outcome before each shot: Before you hit each shot, and particularly if you are faced with a difficult one, say to yourself that you will deal with it wherever it may go. This will help you let go of the shot, and play with more freedom and less tension.

The Use of Statistics

Using stats doesn't sound very exciting, but it can give you an unbiased view of how good your game is, and where you need to focus your practice time. This approach is much as a business would provide accounts in order to give some evidence to show how well it is performing. Evidence is the key word, because you need some proof of how well you are performing if you are to make improvements in your game. The amount of detail needed can vary depending on the level you are playing at, and should only focus on a number of key performance areas. It is possible to over-analyse using statistics, and these should never be too much of a focus while you are playing the game.

- *Fairways hit:* Find out how many fairways per round you are hitting, and note whether you are missing them to the left or to the right.

- *Greens hit in regulation:* A regulation green will be on the green in one on a par 3, two on a par 4 and three on a par 5. Note the greens missed to see if there is a pattern to where they are being missed.
- *Proximity to the hole:* On the greens that you do hit in regulation, note how far away from the hole you are in feet. This will give you an indication as to how far away you are for birdies, because the closer the ball is to the hole, the more likely it becomes that it will convert for a birdie.
- *Putts per round:* Record the number of putts per round that you have on the green.
- *Birdie conversion:* The number of birdies made on holes where a green in regulation is hit.
- *Scrambling:* The number of times when a green is missed that you get up and down to save a par.
- *Sand saves:* The number of times that you are in a bunker and get down in two to save a par.
- *Stroke average:* This is your average score, which will be different to your handicap and will give an indication of your average score.
- *Number of penalties per round:* Where a penalty shot is added due to a lost ball or hitting into a hazard.

This table will give you an indication as to what level each area of your game is at, compared to the level that you aspire

Statistic	Sub 90	Sub 80	European Tour
Fairways hit	38%	54%	68%
Greens in regulation	14%	33%	70%
Proximity to the hole	36ft	30ft	18ft
Putts per round	35	32	29
Birdie conversion	12%	16%	30%
Scrambling	18%	29%	56%
Sand saves	10%	19%	59%
Stroke average	89	79	69.5
Penalties per round	1.7	0.2	0.1

(*Source:* EuropeanTour.com, Strokesaver.com and Strokeaverage.com)

Have a club that is not your driver that you can hit the fairway with.

to. This will show you where you need to make improvements, and where you need to focus your practice time. If you improve in one or more of these areas, this should result in an improvement in your score.

You can record this information in a number of ways because there are numerous statistical packages on the market that you can use. Or you could use a spreadsheet or a paper method. By spending ten minutes going over your round you will be able to review what you did well, and what you need to improve going forwards, and you will start to see some patterns that will give you a clear focus as to how you can improve. This will be valuable information you can share

and discuss with your coach in order to refine your plan of improvement. You will also be able to track your improvement over time, which again will give you evidence that your game is improving, and give you confidence.

Course Management

Managing yourself around the golf course is a way you can learn to save shots. Like anything else you have to make decisions on the golf course, and the success you have will depend on the quality of these decisions. A bad swing won't necessarily result in a bogey, but a bad decision definitely will. Below are some simple

guidelines to help you when you are next on the course.

Have a club that is not your driver that you can get in play: It is great when you are hitting your driver well, but some days it doesn't work, and on a lot of courses you play you won't need a driver on every drive. So it is important to have another club you feel confident you can keep in play: whether it is a 3 wood, 5 wood, hybrid or long iron, it is up to you.

It's OK to hit bad shots, just don't hit two in a row: A big number on a hole isn't the result of one bad swing – what happens is that one bad shot is followed up by another, causing the big number. The late great Seve Ballesteros did hit a lot of wayward drives, but what made him great was that his next shot was often excellent, and he rarely followed up his initial bad shot with another. You may decide when you hit into the trees that you chip out instead of going for a hero shot, because it is up to each individual to assess their own ability to recover from a bad shot. A good guide is only to try the shot if you feel you could play it successfully seven out of ten times or more.

The middle of the green gets you surprisingly close to the pin: If the flag is on the side of the green, consider aiming to the middle. If you miss the green on the side of the green that the pin is on, you will have a lot harder shot to recover, whereas aiming for the middle of the green will give you more of a margin for error, especially on longer shots over 150 yards. Inside that distance you can go for the pin, depending on your skill level and the situation. This strategy works well on par 3 holes where a par is always a good score.

Know how far you hit each club: Working out how far you hit each club will help you massively. Start off working out what you hit from the 100 yard marker, the 150 yards marker, and how far you realistically hit your driver. The popularity of range finders and GPS can also help you work out these distances. These will also change depending on the weather conditions. Once you know these you can make some informed decisions on which bunkers you can carry, how much of the dogleg you should cut

	Carry Distance in Yards
Driver	
3 wood	
5 wood	
3 iron	
4 iron	
5 iron	
6 iron	
7 iron	
8 iron	
9 iron	
PW	
GW	
LW	

Work out how far you hit each club.

off, and which club you should be using. Write these distances down so you can refer to them.

Identify the danger holes and come up with a strategy: Each course has some tough holes where par or even bogey is a good score. The stroke index is a good guide and helps you to work out how best to play these holes. Use your handicap and if you have a stroke on a tough par 4 think of it as par 5 and aim to get on in three shots. Don't be over-ambitious and you can make your birdies on the easier holes.

Look back on your round and identify if your mistakes were a bad swing or bad decision, and ask yourself what you will do in that situation next time. It is important to learn from your mistakes, so after each round spend five minutes reviewing it. Look at your scorecard and maybe go through your stats for the round. Think what you did well and what you could do better, so you can learn when you are in that situation next time. You could even talk through different situations with your coach to ask his opinion about what you should do.

EQUIPMENT

The following objectives are discussed in this chapter:

- To understand why custom-fitted clubs can help your game
- To learn what you need to look for to find the best performing irons, wedges, putters and woods for you

Choosing the equipment that is suited to your game is important, and can have a huge impact on your performance. There are many different options in golf clubs available, so it is important to have some background information about what you should be looking for so you get clubs that will perform for you.

Custom-fitted Golf Clubs

When buying a new set of clubs it is important to get a set that is correct for you and your current ability. Different clubs have different specifications and performance characteristics, and if you get the correct combination for you, this will help your game – and of course, everyone is different. When buying a new set of clubs it is very easy to be custom fitted, and this should be part of the process. This should include a PGA professional discussing your needs and ability so that a number of options can be recommended and you can then try these options. This process should take less than an hour, and if you get the fitting correct you have a better chance of the clubs performing well, which will mean you will enjoying hitting them much more. This will also be more cost effective in the long run, because by getting your clubs custom fitted they will perform better for you, and you are less likely to change them.

It is also important to decide on your budget, how much you play, and your current level. Thus before you get your clubs fitted, be sure to tell the person conducting your fitting what your current ability is. If you are a beginner and are not sure how much you are going to play you will not necessarily require high-end equipment, and may be able to play well with a mid-range option. If you are a serious player, on the other hand, you may

Identify which head shape works best for you.

Get the correct lie: these clubs are, from top, correct, too flat and too upright.

require a higher performing club, which may cost more.

By understanding a few of the ideas given below you will be able to make an informed decision about the most suitable clubs to buy.

Irons

The Correct Head Shape for You

There are different shaped heads that offer different performance characteristics. The bigger head will be much more forgiving and easier to get in the air, as opposed to a smaller head which may be harder to hit but will have more playability. There are also different materials that offer different characteristics and feel.

Length

The correct length is essential so that you can get consistent contact in the middle of the club and have the correct posture. Clubs can be ordered at longer than standard, and the correct length should consider your wrist-to-floor measurement and not just your height. If you are tall this does not automatically mean that you require longer clubs.

Lie Angle

The lie angle is the angle that the club sits to the ground, and this can be adjusted to suit each player. The aim is to have the club contact the ground in a flat position at impact, because if it is too upright or too flat it will cause the clubface to twist, resulting in an offline shot. This is established by hitting some shots from a lie board with tape on the bottom of the club to determine the strike pattern. Marks too close to the toe signal a club that is too flat, which will result in shots to the right, and marks too close to the heel indicate that the club is too upright and will produce shots to the left.

Shaft Type and Flex

The shaft is the most important part of the club to get correct as this can have the most effect on the dispersion of your shots. First you must decide if you want

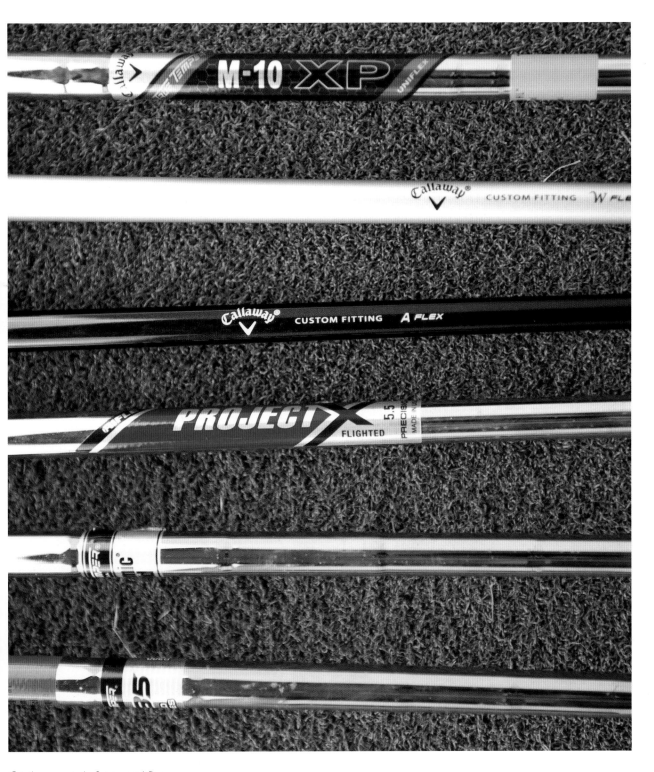

Get the correct shaft type and flex.

graphite or steel shafts. Graphite is much lighter, which will enable you to swing the club faster, a factor that may suit junior, senior and lady golfers better. However, by going for graphite you may sacrifice accuracy over control.

The next consideration is the flex of the shaft, where you can choose from senior flex (A), ladies (L), regular (R), stiff (S) and extra stiff (X) shafts. The stiffer the flex, the less movement there is in the shaft. The flex of the shaft is the ability of the shaft to bend as forces are applied to it in the swing. If the flex is incorrect it will be much more difficult to square the club up to the ball in the swing. A basic guide to what shaft flex you will need is to find out how far you hit your driver in normal conditions. Many people exaggerate this, so make an honest assessment. If you hit

your driver 250 yards or more go with stiff, 220 to 250 you may need a regular, 200 to 220 a senior shaft and 200 yards or less a ladies'. If you are beginning or learning the game, go with a more flexible shaft. Also, when getting fitted try all the different shafts because you will quickly discover what performs best for you.

Grip Type and Size

There are numerous grip types to choose from, every one of which has a different feel. Try them out and experiment until you find one that is comfortable for you. The correct grip size is also very important and can be manipulated to the size of your hands either by ordering larger or smaller grips or by adding extra tape under the grip. To find the correct grip size, take the grip in your left hand

and the fingers should rest against the base of the palm of your hand. If the grip is too small this will encourage excess hand movement in the shot, while too thick a grip will cause insufficient hand movement in the shot.

Wedges

Your wedges are a key club in your bag as they are the scoring clubs and you will be using them for your shots close to the green which have the greatest potential for saving you strokes. The wedges should closely match the rest of your irons in terms of shaft and lie. Many players who play cavity back irons may switch to a more blade style as these clubs give more feel and feedback on shorter shots.

Choose the correct grip type and size for you.

Be sure to have the correct loft progression in your wedges.

The Correct Loft Progression

In order to have wedges that cover the different distances that you face, it is important that you have wedges that have an even gap in your distances. There should be a 4- to 6-degree gap so that your wedges complement each other. The most popular loft progressions are a 48-degree pitching wedge, a 54-degree and a 60-degree, or a 47-, 52- and 58-degree. You can adjust these lofts slightly to your own preference, but ensure you don't have too big a gap between them. Each wedge should have a 15 to 20yd gap between them on a standard full shot.

Drivers

Many golfers would like to hit the ball further, and one way to ensure that you are getting the most you can is to have a correctly fitted driver. A well fitted driver will also reduce the dispersion of your shots and can have a big impact on your game.

Get Fitted on a Launch Monitor

A launch monitor is a piece of equipment that tracks the ball and gives you information on the performance of your shot. This information can be interpreted by a qualified fitter to determine if you are getting the most out of your driver. It will give you information regarding your club head speed, ball speed, launch angle, spin rate, carry distance and total distance, plus how accurate your shots are. A qualified fitter will then be able to see how well your driver is performing for you, and can suggest if there is a better fitting driver that will perform better for you. You will receive tangible numbers that will show you how much better a new driver will perform for you, which increases the probability that you are choosing the correct combination instead of making a guess at which driver will suit you best.

A launch monitor will give you data about what is the best driver for you.

The Correct Loft and Launch Angle

One of the most important elements of a correctly fitting driver is to get the correct loft, which will help you get the best possible initial launch angle of your shot. A good way to think of this is to imagine you are watering your back garden with a hose, with the aim of getting the water to go as far as you can. If you have the hose at too low an angle it will not reach its maximum distance, and the same if you hold it too high. There is a roughly correct angle that will optimize the distance that you can get the water. The same principle holds true for getting the most out of your driver, and having the correct loft will help you maximize distance. It is usually better to have a higher loft than too little. Again, if you are fitted correctly your fitter will be able to give you correct feedback on this.

The Correct Shaft

There are numerous shafts that you can choose from, all of which perform and feel different. The first thing you need to find is one of the correct flex, then the main element that the shaft will affect is the spin rate of the ball. If the ball spins too much it will shoot upwards, too little and it will not stay in the air, both of which will cost you distance. Again, a good fitter will recognize this, aided by the launch monitor. Try different shafts and see which one performs the best by a process of elimination. This is much easier recently due to the advent of heads and shafts that can be screwed and unscrewed, which makes it much easier to try different combinations of head and shaft. Aim to find a shaft you like the feel of, and which performs for you.

Putters

When choosing a putter there are numerous styles, shapes and materials that you can choose from, all of which will feel and perform slightly differently for you. When making your decision ensure that you try several different putters, to find a style that you like and feels good for you. However, there are a few things to keep in mind when making your decision, as described below.

The Correct Length

Putters come in different lengths and can have a big effect on the stroke. The correct length will let your hands hang in a natural position and allow you to get your eyes over the ball. To find the correct putter length, bend forwards from the waist and let your arms hang. Then grip the putter in that position and with the hands still in that natural position. If there is any of the putter grip above that then the putter is too long for you; any lower and it is too short.

The Correct Lie

The putter should also sit flat on the ground and have the correct lie. This can be easily manipulated on most putters and will make it easier to square the clubface through the shot.

Face-Balanced or Blade-Style

If you hold a putter in your hand horizontally you will notice that different

Establishing the correct length of putter: if there is any putter above your grip this means you need a shorter putter; too much below and you need a longer one.

ABOVE & RIGHT: The correct lie of the putter, where it sits flat on the ground as opposed to being too upright or flat.

BELOW: A face-balanced putter will hang with the toe level, as opposed to a blade-style putter where the toe hangs down.

putters hang differently. A mallet-style putter will hang with the face level with the ground: this is known as a face-balanced putter. In a blade-style putter the toe will hang more to the ground. This means that a more face-balanced putter will not tend to rotate as much, whereas a putter with more hang will tend to open in the swing more like a door on a hinge. Experiment with both kinds of putter to see which you prefer.

The Correct Set Make-up

The last element of a correctly fitted set is to have the correct set make-up so that each club has its own job, and you will have a club for the different circumstances that you will face on the course. Also, you are only allowed by the rules to have fourteen clubs in the bag, which means each club's use needs to be maximized.

The correct set make-up is an essential part of any fitting.

Have an even gap between clubs: Each club should have its own job and should go a different distance from other clubs in your bag in normal conditions.

Hit all your clubs on a launch monitor to find your distances: Another advantage of launch monitors is that you can get information about all your clubs and not just the driver. If you hit all your clubs it will give you information about how far they all go, and if, for example, you have two clubs that go the same distance, you may want to consider taking one of them out of the bag.

Examples of set make-ups:

- Driver, 3 wood, 19-degree hybrid, 3 iron to PW, 52-degree wedge, 58-degree wedge, putter
- Driver, 3 wood, 5 wood, 21-degree hybrid, 24-degree hybrid, 5 iron to PW, 54-degree wedge and 60-degree wedge

FURTHER INFORMATION

Further Reading

Carvell, Chic *Fit for Golf*
Hardy, Jim *The Plane Truth*
Hogan, Ben *The Five Fundamentals of Golf*
Morris, Karl *The Golfer's Mind*
Murphy, Michael *Golf in the Kingdom*
Nillson, Pia and Marritott, Lynn *Every Shot Must Have a Purpose*
Penick, Harvey *The Little Red Golf Book*
Rotella, Bob *Golf is not a Game of Perfect*
Woods, Tiger *How I Play Golf*

Useful Contacts and Websites

Professional Golfer Association: www.pga.info
Titleist Performance Institute: www.mytpi.com
The Golf Foundation: www.golf-foundation.org
The English Golf Union: www.englandgolf.org
The European Tour: www.europeantour.com
Scoresaver: www.scoresaver.co.uk
Aimpoint Green reading: www.aimpoint.co.uk

INDEX

OTHER CROWOOD SPORTS GUIDES

CROWOOD SPORTS GUIDES
TRIATHLON
SKILLS · TECHNIQUES · TACTICS

Steve Trew

CROWOOD SPORTS GUIDES
MOUNTAIN BIKING
SKILLS · TECHNIQUES · TRAINING

James McKnight

CROWOOD SPORTS GUIDES
SWIMMING
TECHNIQUE · TRAINING · COMPETITION STRATEGY

Alan Lynn

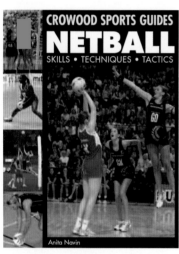

CROWOOD SPORTS GUIDES
NETBALL
SKILLS · TECHNIQUES · TACTICS

Anita Navin

CROWOOD SPORTS GUIDES
MARATHON
AND HALF-MARATHON RUNNING
SKILLS · TECHNIQUES · TRAINING

Steve Trew

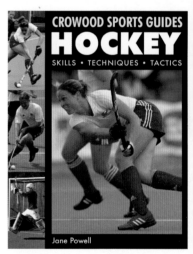

CROWOOD SPORTS GUIDES
HOCKEY
SKILLS · TECHNIQUES · TACTICS

Jane Powell

CROWOOD SPORTS GUIDES
ORIENTEERING
SKILLS · TECHNIQUES · TRAINING

Carol McNeill

CROWOOD SPORTS GUIDES
GYMNASTICS
SKILLS · TECHNIQUES · TRAINING

Lloyd Readhead

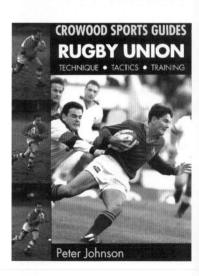

CROWOOD SPORTS GUIDES
RUGBY UNION
TECHNIQUE · TACTICS · TRAINING

Peter Johnson